Twayne's United States Authors Series

Sylvia E. Bowman, *Editor*

INDIANA UNIVERSITY

Robert Nathan

ROBERT NATHAN

By CLARENCE K. SANDELIN

California State College at Los Angeles

Twayne Publishers, Inc.   ::   New York

For

CHARLOTTE

MARSHA, SHARON, KENNETH

Preface

ROBERT NATHAN is the author of more than fifty volumes of fiction, verse, drama, and droll speculation about our human condition. His literary forte is ironic fantasy, typically expressed in short novels which rely on melodic prose, familiar argument, and ingenuous sympathy to evoke in us a sense of the painful beauty and lonely privilege in all mortal experience. The profound simplicity of his storytelling has won him a wide and loyal audience over the years. His first book appeared in 1920; by 1933 his fiction was finding a frequent place on best-seller lists, while Nathan himself was regularly mentioned in the book pages of our metropolitan press; and since then several of his novels have been translated into a dozen modern languages. Still active today, he continues to produce a new book each year.

His popularity with the reading public is matched by his popularity within the writing fraternity. During the three decades he spent in New York City he was deeply involved in literary affairs of the day, and came to know most of the professional writers, publishers, and reviewers who came together there in the years between the two world wars. Not surprisingly, therefore, when John Galsworthy opened an American branch of the international P.E.N. in New York one of the charter members was Robert Nathan; some years later, Nathan served a crucial term as president of this American Center. In 1935 he was elected to the National Institute of Arts and Letters; he is today a Chancellor of the Academy of American Poets. During World War II he held an appointment to the Advisory Council of the Writers War Board; in more recent years he has served on the Board of the Huntington-Hartford Foundation.

In the light of such popular and professional rapport, which he has enjoyed for more than half a century, one may ask why serious critics have not given Nathan more attention. Perhaps some mistrust his simplistic faith in man, country, and God; certainly modern critics have a penchant for rejecting many of the values and visions of yesterday. Others may think him out of touch with contemporary trends; Nathan clearly does not belong, for example, to the fashionable circle of American writers who represent their Jewish heritage in the image of a victim and who think that that victim serves as prototype for all modern, alienated, stateless, faithless men. And no doubt some critics are put off by Nathan's gentle spirit, for in a time of unremitting war it is easy to suspect a writer who still employs the benevolent tone of Saint Francis of Assisi—a writer who scorns the violence of Naturalism, the absurdity of Existentialism, the ruthless metaphysics of most other sexus-nexus-plexus literary creeds. What seems still more likely, however, is that critics accustomed to the gothic rhetoric of Joyce, the sophisticated sensibility of Eliot, and the disenchanted logic of Camus, simply cannot abide the deliberate naïveté of Nathan's art.

But they also serve who only reaffirm the elemental truths, the common joys, the familiar pain and irony of the human condition. Up to now, at least, the popular storyteller has been honored for preserving within his tales the conventional wisdom of his people. While Nathan is more than a modern minstrel, he does resemble those ancient bards and prophets who also addressed their audience *en masse* with dignity, purpose, grace, and wit. He adapts many ancient modes to modern use, but always seeks to preserve and foster what men have cherished for countless generations, and in this fashion he exhibits a literary method all his own for making wise the simple.

Quite obviously no condescension is intended in any reference to Nathan as a popular writer. It is true that the lurid formula fiction illuminating our supermarkets is often called popular fiction and the wooden allegories nailed together by such craftsmen as Horatio Alger, Jr., Charles M. Sheldon, and Edward L. Wheeler are sometimes called popular art; but in truth most of this gross or homiletic nonsense is subliterary. In this study, at any rate, the term *popular writer* is intended to evoke memories of such authors as Washington Irving, John Greenleaf Whittier, Brete Harte, Stephen Vincent Benét, James Thurber, Robert Benchley, and Sinclair Lewis—writers who made no great effort to be in the *avant garde,* but who were content to deal in common modes with common human experience.

The purpose of this study is to examine Nathan's characteristic premises, literary patterns, verbal texture, pervasive tone, and fictional personae in an effort to discover the real nature of his literary achievement. And, since neither biography nor history will be our immediate concern, the principal focus is on his text. All of his book-length works will be examined, and the best of his short prose and characteristic verse come under scrutiny. Every bit of his published verse has in fact been duly inspected, but since Nathan is wont to collect his verse from time to time in books, and in each instance winnows his entire production to preserve what he thinks best, it has been possible to concentrate in this study on verse included in his latest comprehensive selection, *The Green Leaf: The Collected Poems of Robert Nathan* (1950). His juvenilia, his private correspondence, his contributions to journalism, his collaboration in unproduced musicals and stage plays, his work on various screenplays for which he sometimes did and sometimes did not earn credit, his musical compositions, his own lyrics and his translations of foreign lyrics to accompany music composed by others, as well as various drafts and manuscripts which remain unfinished or unpublished, are treated only when they seem relevant to published work.

Thus far no biography of Robert Nathan has appeared, but Dan H. Laurence, whose meticulous documentation in *Robert Nathan: A Bibliography* (1960) makes that volume definitive within its province, has shown real sympathy for Nathan's metier and milieu in various informal essays. Stanley Trachtenberg offers in "Robert Nathan's Fiction" (New York University dissertation, 1963) the first substantial assessment of a purely literary sort, and since most previous comment tends to be cursory, his critical emphasis provides an important corrective. Nevertheless, as a consequence of this limited range of critical dialogue no consensus has yet developed regarding the man and his work, so each new study of Nathan must be presented with appropriate diffidence.

I am especially grateful to Robert Nathan for granting me several interviews during the time when this study was in preparation, and for permitting the liberal quotation from both manuscripts and published work needed to suggest the melodic language, unpredictable fantasy, and humane sensibility which characterize his art. I am also indebted to Geneva Johnson, Irene Russell, Paul Graning, and Frederick B. Shroyer for help, advice, and encouragement.

—CLARENCE K. SANDELIN

California State College
at Los Angeles

Acknowledgments

To Duffield and Company and to Robert Nathan for permission to paraphrase and quote from *Peter Kindred* (copyright 1920).

To Alfred A. Knopf, Inc., and to Robert Nathan for permission to paraphrase and quote from works listed just below. Quotations from *One More Spring* (1933), *Jonah, or The Withering Vine* (1934), *Road of Ages* (1935), *Selected Poems* (1935), *The Enchanted Voyage* (1936), *Winter in April* (1938), *The Barly Fields: A Collection of Five Novels by Robert Nathan* with an Introduction by Stephen Vincent Benét (1938) which contains the previously published *The Fiddler in Barly* and *The Woodcutter's House* and *The Bishop's Wife* and *The Orchid* and *There Is Another Heaven, Journey of Tapiola* (1938), *Portrait of Jennie* (1940), *A Winter Tide* (1940), *They Went on Together* (1941), *Tapiola's Brave Regiment* (1941), *Dunkirk* (1941), *The Sea-Gull Cry* (1942), *Journal for Josephine* (1943), *But Gently Day* (1943), *Morning in Iowa* (1944), *The Darkening Meadows* (1945), *Mr. Whittle and the Morning Star* (1947), *Long After Summer* (1948), *The River Journey* (1949), *The Green Leaf: The Collected Poems of Robert Nathan* (1950), *The Married Look* (1950), *The Innocent Eve* (1951), *Jezebel's Husband* and *The Sleeping Beauty* (1953), *The Train in the Meadow* (1953), *Sir Henry* (1955), *The Rancho of Little Loves* (1956), *So Love Returns* (1958), *The Snowflake and the Starfish* (1959), *The Color of Evening* (1960), *The Weans* (1960), *The Wilderness Stone* (1961), *A Star in the Wind* (1962), *The Married Man* (1962), *The Devil WITH Love* (1963), *The Fair* (1964), *The Mallot Diaries* (1965), *Juliet in Mantua* (1966), and *Stonecliff* (1967) by Robert Nathan are copyrighted and are reprinted by permission of the publisher, Alfred A. Knopf, Inc.

To Robert M. McBride & Company and to Robert Nathan for permission to paraphrase and quote from *Autumn* (copyright 1921).

To *Proceedings of the American Antiquarian Society,* and to Hamilton Vaughan Bail and Robert Nathan, respectively, for permission to quote Robert Nathan, "Letter on History of *Peter*

Contents

Chronology

1894   Robert Gruntal Nathan born January 2, in New York City, to Harold Nathan and Sarah (Gruntal) Nathan. Child a direct descendant of Rabbi Gersham Seixas, one of the eighteenth-century incorporators of Columbia College; and a nephew of Maud Nathan, founder of Consumer's League; and a nephew of Annie (Nathan) Meyer, founder of Barnard College.

1912   After private schooling at home and in Switzerland, and upon graduation from Phillips Exeter Academy, enters Harvard; active there as a cellist, light-weight boxer, fencer, and editor of *Harvard Monthly*. Leaves Harvard without a degree in 1915 to get married.

1915   Begins work in New York advertising agency, and during next five years publishes light essays, verse, and dramatic sketches in metropolitan papers and magazines while completing four book-length manuscripts.

1920   *Peter Kindred,* his first book, a *Bildungsroman.* Moves to California for approximately a year.

1921   Returns to New York, becomes active in literary life of Greenwich Village. *Autumn,* his first fable in fantasy, establishes pattern of short novel he characteristically employs thereafter.

1922   *Youth Grows Old,* a volume of verse.

1923   *The Puppet Master,* short novel.

1925   Offers instruction (1924-25) in verse-writing at New York University School of Journalism. *Jonah,* his best early achievement in the short novel of fantasy.

1926   *The Fiddler in Barly,* short novel.

1927   *The Woodcutter's House,* short novel.

1928   *The Bishop's Wife,* short novel; in 1947 made into a motion picture starring Cary Grant, Loretta Young, David Niven.

1929   *A Cedar Box,* a volume of verse. *There Is Another Heaven,* short novel.

1931   *The Orchid,* short novel.

1933   *One More Spring,* short novel; deals with economic crisis of 1930's. His first great popular success; in 1935 made into a motion picture starring Warner Baxter, Janet Gaynor. Nathan publishes "On Being a Jew," *Scribner's*.

1935   *Road of Ages*, short novel; deals with hypothetical expulsion of Jews from all civilized countries. Nathan elected to National Institute of Arts and Letters. *Selected Poems*.

1936   *The Enchanted Voyage*, short novel; in 1946 made into a motion picture ("Wake Up and Dream") starring June Haver, John Payne, Charlotte Greenwood.

1938   *Winter in April*, short novel. *Journey of Tapiola*, tale of fantasy.

1940   *Portrait of Jennie*, short novel, probably his best known work of fiction; in 1948 made into a picture starring Jennifer Jones, Joseph Cotten, Ethel Barrymore. *A Winter Tide*, a volume of verse.

1941   *They Went on Together*, short novel. *Dunkirk*, a ballad.

1942   *The Sea-Gull Cry*, short novel.

1943   *Journal for Josephine*, memoir of author's experience on Cape Cod during World War II. *But Gently Day*, short novel.

1944   *Morning in Iowa*, panegyric in narrative verse in the manner of Stephen Vincent Benét.

1945   *The Darkening Meadows*, a volume of verse.

1947   *Mr. Whittle and the Morning Star*, short novel; deals with implications of nuclear holocaust.

1948   *Long After Summer*, short novel.

1949   *The River Journey*, short novel.

1950   *The Green Leaf: The Collected Poems of Robert Nathan*. *The Married Look*, short novel. *The Adventures of Tapiola*, tale of fantasy.

1951   *The Innocent Eve*, short novel; his most bitter indictment of contemporary human behavior.

1953   *Jezebel's Husband* and *The Sleeping Beauty*, two dramatic pieces published in single volume; *Jezebel's Husband*, a play written in 1951-52, was first performed at Pocono Playhouse, Mountainhome, Pa., on August 4, 1952; *The Sleeping Beauty*, a play written in 1949.

1955   *Sir Henry*, short novel.

1956   *The Rancho of Little Loves*, short novel.

1958   *So Love Returns*, short novel.

1959   *The Snowflake and the Starfish*, tale of fantasy for children.

1960   *The Color of Evening,* short novel. *The Weans,* thin volume of mock-scholarship designed to lampoon modern Americans; subject ironically identified as "Archeology" by the author.

1961   *The Wilderness Stone,* a semi-autobiographical short novel; includes a fictionized account of author during his salad years in literary New York.

1962   *A Star in the Wind,* a full-length novel almost devoid of Nathan's customary fantasy; deals with the struggle to establish the modern state of Israel; though less intricate in imaginative design, it defines many of author's most characteristic attitudes and beliefs, and it is perhaps his most convincing work of fiction. *The Married Man,* a volume of light verse.

1963   *The Devil* WITH *Love,* short novel.

1964   *The Fair,* short novel.

1965   *The Mallot Diaries,* short novel.

1966   *Juliet in Mantua,* a play; provides alternative ending to Shakespeare's tragedy which converts it into situation comedy.

1967   *Stonecliff,* short novel; semi-autobiographical account of how fantasy based on feeling involves its author and the audience. Also illustrates the unflagging productivity of an author who has produced a new book every year since **1920.**

CHAPTER 1

Ours Was a Generation Set Apart

THERE have been many eruptions of creative energy in American letters. One of the first occurred in the decade before the Civil War when masterpieces by Ralph Waldo Emerson, Nathaniel Hawthorne, Herman Melville, Henry David Thoreau, and Walt Whitman suddenly appeared. Not until the twentieth century did this country feel such shocks again; then, just as Americans were winning World War I, and losing the peace it promised, fresh tremors of creative force were felt. In the three decades from 1900 to 1929, Henry Adams, Robert Frost, Eugene O'Neill, T. S. Eliot, Ernest Hemingway, F. Scott Fitzgerald, and William Faulkner—to cite obvious examples—all published major works. For the most part, however, this fresh energy went into lateral thrusts, at random intervals, cracking the molds of genteel provinciality, shaking a moribund theater into life, driving poets into new structures of meaning, opening fresh spaces for small publishers, and making the literate public curious about the grounds of national culture.

Robert Nathan, who began writing in this period, relished this literary and intellectual excitement. Living and working in the very center of creative activity in New York, he eagerly joined and supported those groups and programs of which he approved, quietly resisted trends he doubted or deplored, and all the while worked to develop his own mode of reaffirming traditional values. Naturalism was then rampant in literature; yet Nathan's forte became the short novel of prose fantasy which seldom employed literal settings, animalistic characters, violent conflict, or any argument that life is meaningless. The ingenuous modern fable he devised in the 1920's relied instead on humbly idyllic place and circumstance, introduced imperfect but always humane men and women, explored the recurrent action of archetypal experience, and projected an uncomplicated faith in the significance of mortal life within that larger mystery of theistic purpose conventionally defined by our Judeo-Christian heritage. It was a cameo form of the novel, deeply conservative as most serious popular literature tends to be; it offered entertainment, confirmation, and consolation.

In the euphoria of the 1920's, however, when so many members of the *avant garde* were advocating more sophisticated theory and practice in drama, poetry, and prose, and when sensitive people in all walks of life were newly conscious of the obligations thrust upon a callow young nation in a world "saved for democracy," Nathan's didactic emphasis, subjective exposition, mystical argument, familiar premises, nostalgic moods, and folkloristic story motifs must have seemed a bit old-fashioned. Although his early books denounce the avarice and alienation fostered by modern materialism, Nathan did not feel any compulsion to become an expatriate, a convert, an anarchist, a feminist, or a psuedo-Freudian. He preferred to stay at home and play the role at hand. His thirty-three short novels, nine books of verse, two longer works of fiction, three published plays, a personal memoir, some mock-scholarship, one tale for children, and his writing for motion pictures serve to illustrate how a popular author may contribute a serious definition of the exoteric moods and meanings which persist within the complex culture of contemporary America.

I *One of the Sad Young Men*

Nathan's first long work of fiction *Peter Kindred* (imprinted 1919, but not published until January 1920) is one of several novels that appeared just after World War I in which the sad young men of a lost generation identified themselves and their dolor. On the heels of Nathan's book came *This Side of Paradise* (1920) by F. Scott Fitzgerald; *Moon-Calf* (1920) by Floyd Dell; and *One Man's Initiation—1917* (1920) by John Dos Passos. The next year *Erik Dorn* (1921) by Ben Hecht and *The Beginning of Wisdom* (1921) by Stephen Vincent Benét appeared. Although Ernest Hemingway published some of his characteristic stories in 1923 and 1924, *The Sun Also Rises*—often thought to mark the high point of this literary tide of youthful introspection and frustration—did not appear until 1926.

Peter Kindred is a semi-autobiographical novel quite frankly based on the author's own early years at Exeter, at Harvard, and in New York City. During his years on campus Nathan served as editor for the *Harvard Monthly*, he made the fencing team, wrote musical reviews for the metropolitan press, met and married Dorothy Michaels. The newlyweds moved to New York City to set up housekeeping.

The fictional account traces the quiet, unsensational development of a sensitive boy's mind and character during his years as student up to his first major encounter with adult disappointment. At the university Peter Kindred earnestly cultivates friends, savors the musical events of campus life, is converted to an economic theory promulgated by a Professor Carver, and ultimately meets Joan, a Radcliffe girl. Peter and Joan form a common-law union and move into a New York City tenement where they try to live in accordance with the rational ideals of Carverian theory, but find that problems of ordinary living can quite overwhelm them and their unsentimental principles. The novel ends with Peter's shock when their child is stillborn.

Some reviewers thought the book was awkwardly paced, distorted perhaps by the author's private nostalgia, and too fastidious in any case for popular taste. But Walter Lippmann, reviewing it for *Current Opinion*, said he liked it and found it authentic. Although he recognized the Harvard represented in the book, Lippmann felt that Nathan's evocation was more disillusioned, more intimate, less public, more sensuous, and less reckless in ideas than the actual Harvard of Lippmann's own experience.

Some forty years after its publication, when asked to furnish data for an article on Harvard fiction which later appeared in the October, 1958, issue of *Proceedings of the American Antiquarian Society,* Nathan offered his own comment on the genesis, publication, reception, and significance of *Peter Kindred*:

> I wrote the book in 1917—the second winter after I had left Harvard (I didn't graduate; I got married instead).
>
> I wrote it while I was in the advertising business in New York and very homesick for Harvard and New England generally. I couldn't find a publisher; the answer always came back the same—if it had been a second book they would have taken it, but a first book was too much of a gamble (things were different in those days!). Finally in 1919 (after I had written two other

books, neither of which has ever been published) Duffield
agreed to bring it out.

I believe that I in turn agreed to give up my royalties on the
first thousand copies. The book was published in January of
1919[1] [sic], at which time I was already working on Autumn.
A thousand copies were printed, of which some nine hundred
something were sold. Scott Fitzgerald's This Side of Paradise
came out about the same time and completely stole the show.
Peter Kindred was never reprinted; its value lies chiefly in its
rarity.

As one might perhaps expect of any Bildungsroman based
chiefly on the author's own experience, Peter Kindred has a personal frame of reference, explores issues which engaged the
interest of many other young writers of Nathan's generation, and
reflects a Romantic temper which persisted in some American
writing during the early decades of the twentieth century. Only
the ancient pattern of a young man's initiation has more universal implications.

The personal frame of reference is implicit in the hypersensi-
tivity of Peter Kindred. Although Nathan explained in the course
of an interview that this particular character is modeled upon
two of his college friends, there is still no mistaking a diffidence
in the fictional personality we also find in the author himself.
Peter "was too aware of the little he had to offer," says the
novelist; "it was not modesty but a true humility" (8). A like
humility characterizes all of Nathan's other heroes, and is repeatedly endorsed in the exposition of book after book in subsequent years. In addition to this humble posture, moreover, are
the mystical moods which characterize Peter's response to the
simple joy and mystery of mortal experience. "It was the sorrow
of youth inarticulate," says the author, "sorrow because the earth
is beautiful" (9). Both this mood and explanation recur many
times in Peter Kindred, and later novels.

Not only the author's habitual modesty and mood, but also the
social circumstances of his private life influence the novel. There
is a secondary character, for instance, the young musician David,
who can never quite escape the age-old, senseless bigotry of
man. Even at Harvard his companions indulge in a polite form of
bitter prejudice. "Oh, I'm not down on Jews as a race," says one
of David's classmates. "There's something . . . a rather pathetic

and wistful sweetness about Jewish women . . . some Jewish women. And some Jewish men have a lot of fire. But this chap David doesn't seem to have found himself . . . a bit volcanic still, and grumbling. Too eager. And then, of course, he's a Jew, and Peter simply can't take him around with him, Don, because the men who like Peter, don't like Jews. I don't blame them . . . they've been brought up that way" (84). Nathan readily admits that he is the model for David, the musician, an introspective spirit, a patient being.

Despite this personal reference, *Peter Kindred* is not purely subjective. It explores many of the issues common to other fiction of the time. Prior to World War I, for example, a naïve myth of progress had served as the dominant premise in nineteenth-century American life, but the campus popularity of such a book as *The Education of Henry Adams*, following its formal publication in 1918, suggests that many intellectuals were ready to repudiate that myth. The new generation of writers not only challenged the old notion of progress, but found precious little else to leave unchallenged in the American scheme of things. Puritanism was condemned for inhibiting joy and imagination, business was denounced for its lack of ethics, cities were scorned as evidence of material success and spiritual failure, marriage was mocked as a surrender to sentimental female domination, and the existing society indicted for its failure to provide real opportunity for independent and creative life.[2] Not surprisingly, perhaps, most of the sad young men depicted in the fiction of the early 1920's seemed to be searching for a father image to replace something they lost during the years of total war and pointless victory.

Peter Kindred is no exception. He repudiates his familiar religion, condemns fraud and greed in business, discovers that an urban jungle exists within New York City, experiments in a love affair shorn of sentimental trappings, and concludes that modern American society does offer very little succor for the spirit of man.

It is the emotional temper of the novel, however, that is most characteristic of both its author and an older mode of story-telling. Nathan is, first and always, a man of feeling. *Peter Kindred* stresses repeatedly the singularity of human consciousness, the isolation of each private personality, and the inevitable loneliness of spirit which therefore attends our human condition. The following vignette from his first novel represents a tone Nathan exploits in nearly all his work.

"Well, mother," he said uncertainly, "shall we open a little wine . . . for the children . . . a little toast to the children, all by ourselves? . . ."

She smiled at him and roused herself. To the south and to the east, far off, the names of her two children were whispered through the darkness and were answered, nor was there, south or east, a thought of these old folk who held their glasses of red wine to the light, and turning toward each other clinked them bravely, and wished their children well. (339-40)

Emotionality of this sort is characteristic of much else that appeared during the first two decades of this century, for it was a time when popular verse and fiction in America still reflected an older Romantic tradition fostered by the likes of Henry Wadsworth Longfellow. Nor was it only David Belasco, Bliss Carman, Clyde Fitch, John Fox, Richard Hovey, Joyce Kilmer, Gene Stratton-Porter, and Booth Tarkington who helped preserve the sentimental syndrome. The frequent bathos, compulsive self-expression, and emotional clichés of even the most serious writers drove Ezra Pound, Gertrude Stein, and T. S. Eliot to formulate their several famous declarations of protest. Yet this emotional emphasis and subjective orientation was not without some twentieth-century apologists among respectable men of letters. One such was the Parisian Anatole France, a controversial literary wit who startled the orthodox by embracing Darwinism, repudiating Christianity, and extolling God at the same time.

By the time Nathan began to write, the literary opinions of Anatole France had become a vogue in America. Among other things, the Frenchman preferred to think that the creative act, precisely because it was so often irrational, subjective, and inspired, could best be defined as a mode of conscious dreaming. In the final chaper of *Le Livre de mon ami* (1885), for example, France insists that dreaming must be the ultimate faculty of man: "Not by the faculty of laughter does man rise above the animals," he says, "but by the gift of dreaming. The storyteller remakes the world after his own fashion, and gives to lesser men, to children, a chance to make it over in theirs."

Sigmund Freud was to formulate a few years later a more

convincing explanation of the link between dreams and crea-
tivity; but, if Anatole France did not offer a full rationale, he did
amply illustrate his subjective method in several novels popular
on both sides of the ocean. That Nathan read many of these
novels with care and admiration would be obvious even if he
had not cheerfully acknowledged it. He borrowed rhetoric from
Anatole France's *Thaïs* for his own story about young Jonah, as
we shall notice later on; and he appropriated most of the characters and a central situation from France's *Le Mannequin d'osier*
for his own New England tale about Henry Pennifer's granddaughter.[3]

There is certainly a dream-haunted quality about *Peter Kindred* that suggests Anatole France had some effect on Nathan
from the beginning. Peter's good friend, the musician David,
dreams of a music that can compass and express the beauty of
the Charles River landscape. Another friend, Jill, feels that to
work and *dream*, to feed the soul richly, is the real life of a student. When young men gather in a Harvard room to gossip, they
seem to wander in a *dream*, along old paths, almost without
effort. Sometimes, when Peter grows especially restless and
lonely, he seeks refuge in the warm oblivion of the Boston
movies where he can buy, "in darkness stirred with music, a sort
of trance, a cessation of his own breathing, living and moving,
and a projection into the untroubled if erratic lives of heroes and
heroines" (49). On one occasion he meets a girl on shipboard
and, after a pleasant evening, in a waking *dream*, they kiss each
other good night. Later on the memory of this tawny woman
drives Peter back to the movies where screen heroines arouse in
him a quiet *dreaminess* of some past happening in his own life,
tenuous and sweet.

Even Peter's reaction to a winter landscape seen at night while
crossing New England on a train takes on a night-mare quality:
"It was a vision of small things, of futile things, a vision of men's
hands blocked and defeated by the still land, of desires groping
for expression, doomed to failure, passion forced to the rut of
living, inarticulate life, gaunt and joyless. It was a vision of men
and maids, of crude loves growing old, of dreams coming to
nothing. Is that why we fear the land, he asked himself, our
dreams coming to nothing?" (141).

Peter even discovers his own love for Joan in the course of a
dream, and his whole emotional complexion changes while he

sleeps. And, as the two lovers plan a future in New York, Peter's eyes *dream* of a tenement and of brave young people loving and working there. The success of their marriage is assessed first in purely subjective terms, and only later in relation to objective experience: "It was entirely as they had dreamed of living, and yet Peter wondered sometimes if it were possible that their dream in its broad sweep had troubled itself too little with Mulligans" (283), those objective figures who inhabit drab reality.

Perhaps the dreamlike quality of the story does suggest the roiling inner experience of Peter Kindred, the lonely, confused, and guileless young man involved for the first time in an adult confrontation of the beauty, mystery, and ruthless force of this world; but the subjective meditations are usually too long and lugubrious. For the most part, the dreams are so repetitive, so scantily related to the overt action and actual circumstances, that Peter's story often bogs down in self-conscious musing. As a consequence, we almost fail to notice that the novel does present the archetypal pattern of a young man's initiation. The first nine chapters certainly seem too desultory and too private for the average reader. There, events of only modest import are presented, we assume, mainly because such things did happen once to the author or his friends and, within the Romantic conception of literature as self-expression, therefore deserve to be rehearsed even if they add little to the imaginative construct. Only when the action of the story shifts away from routine life at Harvard does bland recitation give way to dramatic invention. In the last three chapters, however, the basic structure becomes clear and meaningful.

Of course Peter's initiation does begin while he is still in school when, as a consequence of abandoning God, he gradually comes to feel an internal tension. His first conscious test involves little more than giving up the comfortable habit of prayer, something Peter finds a bit disconcerting, but which also represents a step toward independence. His next major test occurs when he and Joan, both impressed by the theories of Professor Carver, decide to form a family union on purely rational principles which supersede the religious conventions of marriage.

Their ultimate test comes, however, when they move to New York and pit their theories against the reality of ordinary metropolitan life. They talk earnestly about the larger welfare of mankind that a pure rationalism should bring to pass, but in the meantime they live frugally in the slums. Peter is obliged to work at humble chores since he can find no employment for his real talents. When Joan also takes a job, the double load of home and work, the drabness of tenement existence, the crippling heat of metropolitan summer, and the shock of street rioting combine to break her health. As a consequence, their child is stillborn. This moment of trauma is the culmination of Peter's initiation, for then he realizes how much he needs a power beyond his own, and how much he hopes for a meaning beyond fate. Unfortunately, he does not know where to find such power and meaning; but his resolve to search for them indicates his mature recognition of the fragile human condition.

Although *Peter Kindred* does not end with explicit religious affirmation, it nevertheless is testamentary fiction. The steady attacks on logic and materialism, the didactic exposition, and the pervasive concern with theism provide ample evidence of Nathan's ethical concern. Yet the novel is no moral tract; the characters are viable, the story has at least a rudimentary structure, and there is dramatic tension in the closing chapters. Thus, even if the early chapters are rather slow in pace and personal in reference, even if the later chapters more often echo than analyze the issues of the day, and even if the tone seems sentimental, the point of view Romantic, and the archetypal pattern of experience only awkwardly defined, the novel does offer an old-fashioned kind of comfort, an affirmation of common verities, a troubled but persistent hope for man, and a deep if paradoxical concern about God.

II *Experiments in Style*

Before Nathan finally left the advertising agency, and while his bulky manuscript of *Peter Kindred* was still suffering the rounds of editorial inspection, Nathan dipped once more into the works of H. G. Wells, Miguel de Cervantes, Jonathan Swift, and Anatole France. What he again found most beguiling was the credible impossibilities of Wells's *The Time Machine,* the gentle sadness behind the firm satire of Cervantes' *Don Quixote,* the meticulous language and moral indignation of Swift's *Gulliver,* and, above all, the verbal splendor and ironic tension of France's *Thaïs.* The reading seems to have helped to extricate him from the literal frame of reference and private rhetoric of *Peter Kindred*, for *The Letters of Fra Rombadille* (a book-length manuscript completed in 1918, but unpublished except for the three excerpts cited below) deals with more universal themes and employs that highly mannered style just then a vogue in such publications as *Smart Set*.

Nathan experiments with credible impossibilities, there is some melancholy satire, his language is melodic if not meticulous, and there is a bit of moralizing as he seeks to blend the fantasy of folktales with the candor of informal essays. He obviously worked hard at developing a style; but, to anyone familiar with the work of Anatole France, the bright mockery, patterned prose, and quaint simplicity would not seem wholly original. A typical passage from *The Concert* (an excerpt from the *Rombadille* manuscript, separately printed in 1940) suggests, indeed, that Nathan comes closer to his French than to his Spanish or English models:

> I was born no more than two and twenty years ago in a little village of a northern province whose intrepid ruler brought down upon himself the wrath of the present Emperor by sneezing in his presence, with the result that he was thrown into prison, and his subjects taxed almost to their last minimum coin. I can still remember the arrival of our runner with the lamentable tidings; he burst into the square like one distraught, and could say nothing until he had been comforted with the best of everything. That day my father returned home with a thoughtful air, and spent the entire evening in company with his wife and two children, and when bed time came for my sister and me, we were allowed to take our old dog to bed with us. How the memories return; my mind is crowded with them. The next day I awoke to hear the tramp of soldiers in the streets, the beating of drums, and the clink and the clatter of spears in the market place.[4]

The narrative burbles on like this, becoming more arabesque with every word, until conventional speech and customary action all but melt into a dream. No doubt formulaic language, exotic settings, bizarre characters, and burlesque events are appropriate to this account of an eighteenth-century monk who, though cast away upon an island off the coast of Africa, can meet there without the least surprise a virtuoso on the ocarina.

Folkloristic mode and mood do help the author to achieve droll understatement, a satire based on diminution, and something like that primeval simplicity of old fables; but his heavy reliance upon exaggerated manner does not always compensate for want of matter. His sustained rhetoric gets monotonous, the cheerful verbal play seldom matures into profound emotion or sophisticated argument, and the melancholy tone seems honest but unjustified by anything within the narrative itself. Amusing in some respects, *The Concert* is too bland and ethereal, too much engrossed in style, still too experimental.

After reading this narrative excerpt from Nathan's *Rombadille* manuscript, we could almost think he had been a party to those esthetic movements in *fin de siècle* Europe, especially since he entered Greenwich Village life just about the time Guido Bruno was campaigning there for Oscar Wilde, Walter Pater, Arthur Symons and others whom Bruno regarded as persecuted literary saints. Anatole France was, of course, an esthetician whom Nathan admired. Yet in another excerpt from the *Rombadille* manuscript, entitled "This Thing Called Art" printed by *The Reviewer* in 1921, Nathan certainly shows no interest in "art for art's sake." The artist, indeed, he says is unique because he "bulges more toward God," and because his estate is swelled with grief, or large with pity: "We mark it in his music, we hear it in his verse, we see it grow beneath his brush. Vistas open before us; we do not see their end; perhaps they are infinite. The artist, poor soul, knows well enough where they end; only the prophet is lost in God."[5] Nathan's emphasis is on the artist's sympathy for man, not on his obligation to art; and the dominant frame of reference is frankly religious rather than esthetic.

In a third excerpt from the *Rombadille* manuscript, entitled "Peter Truffle Meditates" when printed by *The Reviewer* in 1922, Nathan suggests that love rather than beauty offers the ultimate secular experience. "Love comes unbidden to us all," observes the ruminant Peter Truffle, "and is a source of sorrow to each one; yet of that memorable host which has suffered because of love there is no one, no matter how profound his grief, who would be better off without it."[6] Perhaps so, but this unsweated retrospection is scarcely what Pater, for one, meant when he spoke of burning with a hard, gemlike flame.

Actually these excerpts from *The Letters of Fra Rombadille* suggest a closer parallel, both in definition and practice, to quite another literary tradition—to a contemporary style shaped by the ancient force of Jewish experience, which differs sharply from the esthetic principles we commonly associate with the Symbolist Movement, say, or with Decadence, or Imagism, or any kindred patterns. For, though he may not have been conscious of it himself, Nathan often employs a style very like that found in Yiddish literature.

Where the typical American story tends to employ a carefully selected patterns of diction and action intended to define, if only by indirection, some climax or epiphany with an economy of force, most Yiddish stories are content to offer an accumulation of sensuous impressions by means of a winding oral narrative or by recounting a small bare story in which the characters are hardly glimpsed, where conflict scarcely exists, and where nothing seems to happen. For what matters most to Yiddish writers, according to Irving Howe,[7] is the context, the contour, the choreography of social behavior that repeats and justifies the collective destiny of the Jews; and the undercurrent of verbal melody becomes the ultimate carrier of meaning to a special audience sensitive to the interplay of mood and meaning, so that the rhythm of a voice—sometimes that of a speaker in the story, sometimes that of the author speaking on his own behalf— is sufficient to establish a deep communion. Events themselves are relatively unimportant except as they identify the recurrent situations, the archetypal predicament, of the Jews. In recognizing these recurrent situations, the audience is reminded of the traditional values generated by Jewish experience, the virtue of powerlessness, for example, and the power of helplessness, the loyalty of the dispossessed, the sanctity of the insulted and the injured.

Not surprisingly the literature sponsored by such a culture has little interest in run-of-the-mill heroes, who are apt to be concerned over their private fortune and who, in Western civilization at any rate, are so often involved in some cult of violence. Not the egoist, but the representative man, not the personal agon, but the continuing mystery of a unique social experience, are the characteristic elements of Yiddish fiction. The protagonist is therefore apt to be some fresh example of the old patriarchal types, or else some long-suffering, persistent, ironic, often poor but proud example of *dos kleine menschele*, the little man, who serves as the anti-heroic agent for all mankind.

Nathan, of course, is not a Yiddish writer. His own cultural antecedents are predominantly Hispanic rather than East European, and his professional writing has always been in English rather than in Yiddish. His family, moreover, has been represented in America since colonial times, and Nathan's personal dedication is to the nation of his birth and to the democratic system which seeks to incorporate all groups without destroying their cultural diversity.

Nevertheless the adumbrations to be found in *Peter Kindred,* as well as stylistic trends and critical speculation in *The Letters of Fra Rombadille,* do suggest many parallels between Nathan's literary mode and that of modern Yiddish writing. It seems quite natural, in fact, that the Jewish heritage might influence the tone, point of view, choice of imagery, and verbal cadences of any writer who had once deeply felt its power.

CHAPTER 2

A Fabulous Ferment

NATHAN had been publishing short prose pieces and individual poems quite regularly after his first arrival in New York. *Smart Set* published "It: The Usual Play with an Unusual Ending" in 1915, and "Atavism: A Tale of Passions in the Rough" in 1916. By 1920 more than a dozen of his poems had appeared in *Smart Set, New York Times, Evening Post, Century, Atlantic Monthly, Everybody's* and *Freeman.* His early prose has happily enough been forgotten, but Nathan has preserved the best of his verse in *The Green Leaf: The Collected Poems of Robert Nathan* (1950).

During his first five years in New York he also completed four book-length manuscripts, finishing the first draft of *Peter Kindred* in 1917; *The Letters of Fra Rombadille* in 1918; *Sweet Peep* (a story he later described as a combination of *Alice in Wonderland* and Wells's *Time Machine*) in 1919; and *Autumn,* his first short novel about rural life in Barly, in 1920. The *Rombadille* and *Sweet Peep* manuscripts, except for the excerpts examined in the previous chapter, remain unpublished.

I *A Medieval Fable*

From the time he finished his first novel Nathan had been searching for some fresh approach, a different format, a distinctive mode of his own. What he finally developed was his version of the short novel, a work of some thirty-five thousand words, in which he largely ignores the conventions of Realistic fiction, and creates a composite form of modern bestiary, moral parable, and secular prophecy. His first publication in this mode is *Autumn* (1921). Along with a volume of verse entitled *Youth Grows Old* (1922) and *Peter Kindred* (1920), this work represented Nathan's major claim to active membership in the new literary generation. The reception of *Autumn,* Nathan's second published work, was cordial. Even so reviewers of a literal turn were annoyed by so much that seemed unconventional. The book, said *Catholic World*, is quite unconvincing—"unreal as a dream, and its conclusion is unsatisfactory and inartistic." There were others, however, who agreed with Carl Van Doren's description of *Autumn* as an all but perfect native pastoral, rural as a farmer's almanac; with language cool and fresh as dew, the novel offered a story—though drenched in reverie—that was supported by shrewd intelligence and affectionate irony.

A candid look at the text itself suggests ample grounds for both reactions. Nathan's opening paragraph, for example, is typical of his new manner: "On Sunday the church bells of Hillsboro rang out across the ripening fields with a grave and holy sound, and again at evening knocked faintly, with quiet sorrow, at doors where children watched for the first star, to make their wishes. Night came, and to the croaking of frogs, the moon rose over Barly Hill. . . ." Here certainly is sonorous verbal beauty, created out of time-rubbed imagery and deftly cadenced prose. Perhaps this much of the paragraph could almost pass for a translation from one of Anatole France's graceful causeries, or some essay from *L'Histoire Comique* where the Frenchman caught the ambient countryside of Rouen in his net of words.

But as Nathan's melody rolls on, it begins to cloy: " . . . In the early morning the grass, still wet with dew, chilled the bare toes of urchins on their way to school where, until four o'clock, the tranquil voice of Mr. Jeminy disputed with the hum of bees, and the far off clink of the blacksmith's forge in the village" (1). Even general readers brought up on Longfellow or Walt Disney must surely find the church bells, wishing star, croaking frogs, rising moon, barefoot urchins, gentle schoolmaster, and village blacksmith entirely too bucolic.

Yet *Autumn* is not without literary precedent. In a modest fashion it almost illustrates William Wordsworth's Romantic theory, for it also deals with situations from common life, which are related in a selection of language really used by men, over which the author throws a certain coloring of the imagination, so that ordinary things appear to the mind in an unusual aspect. And in such work Nathan does seek to trace the primary laws of our nature. A parallel approach does not, of course, insure a parallel achievement. Nathan's fable owes less to Romantic than to medieval precedent in any case, for *Autumn* is essentially an adaptation of *The Little Flowers of Saint Francis*.

Frankly seeking to recapture the simple piety, sentimental tone, and fantastic perspective of the original parables of Brother Francis, *Autumn* is a tale of elemental life in a rural New England village where the schoolmaster, one Mr. Jeminy, observes that youth is not without courage nor age without wisdom, but that those who are rich quarrel with the poor, and the poor with the rich—and also with each other; for every man reaches for more, like a child at table. This selfish and materialistic obsession explains why, Mr. Jeminy feels, there is today such poverty of heart, of mind, and of spirit. As a teacher, he steadily opposes these gross attitudes, but with no success; therefore he is often reduced to making private songs:

> Laws, manuals,
> And texts incline us
> To cheat with plus
> And rob with minus.[1]

Mr. Jeminy draws his own inspiration from a lifetime spent in studying the King James version of the Bible, the first-century Stoicism of Epictetus, the third-century Neo-Platonism of Plotinus, the fifth-century consolation of Boethius, the thirteenth-century humility of Saint Francis, and the sixteenth-century humor—at once so gentle, yet so austere—of Cervantes. From all this study he distills a modest definition of the good life. "Love," he says, "peace, the quiet of the heart, the work of one's hands. Perhaps it is human to wish for more. But to be human is not always to be wise" (182). No doubt his argument is reductive, his reference selective, his vision simplistic, yet all of this would be in character for one who purports to function as a modern Saint Francis. And in the book Mr. Jeminy's attitude of innocence does serve to rebuke our modern sophistication, for it bespeaks a simple unity that few men today still feel.

But the novel also differs from its model. Nathan's twentieth-century pastoral often employs the animism found in its thirteenth-century antecedent, but there is a substantial difference in method and effect. The creature world surrounding Francis of Assisi serves to discover and define his vision of universal love, but the one surrounding Mr. Jeminy often reflects and confirms his disappointment with a greedy and aggressive way of life: "Mr. Jeminy turned down toward the village, where he had an errand to attend to. As his footsteps died away, the minnows swam back again, as though nothing had happened. One, larger than the rest, found a piece of bread which had fallen into the water. 'This is my bread,' he said, and gazed angrily at his friends, who were trying to bite him. 'I deserve the bread,' he added" (3).

And this satirical temper, of course, is still another way in which Nathan's story differs from its medieval prototype. Human folly is frequently subjected here to ridicule. Practical Mr. Frye, who keeps the general store and runs the village post office, provides a case study in materialism. He sees his neighbors, for example, in the form of fruits, vegetables, stick pins, and pieces of calico; and, when he looks at young Anna Barly, the girl his son loves, he sees only acres of land, live stock, farm buildings, and money in the bank. Nor is he the only one of his type. Equally afflicted with greed is Mr. Crabbe, who manages to make his point of view offensive. "The way I look at it," he says quite candidly, "It's like this: first, there's me; and then there's you" (44).

Against such deep-grained attitudes old Mr. Jeminy can make no progress. He had come to the town full of plans and hope; he was intent on teaching that happiness comes not from owning much, but from needing little since riches bring trouble that crowds love out of the heart. But not one of all whom he taught reading, writing, and arithmetic grows up to be better or happier. These people of Barly seem, in fact, very like the sparrows that fly up in noisy protest whenever he spades ordure into the garden soil; they are annoyed at him for interrupting even for a moment their ravenous grubbing.

"Come," he is then wont to say to the greedy, squalling, heedless birds, "the world does not belong to you. I believe you have never read the works of Epictetus, who says, 'true education lies in learning to distinguish what is ours from what does not belong to us.' However, you have a more modern spirit; for you believe that whatever you see belongs to you, providing you are able to get hold of it" (98). This parable that smells of the lamp is strangely spiced with satire, and yet it is Franciscan in its simple deprecation of the modern corporality of life. Sparrows, minnows, and New Englanders are all depicted as the victims of a base acquisitive instinct that keeps them forever scavengers and hoarders, bereft of peace and love, engrossed in material things, and dead in spirit.

Of course Nathan was not alone in making such an indictment of modern America. *Autumn* was published in 1921; in 1922 T. S. Eliot defined *The Waste Land*, Sinclair Lewis introduced *Babbitt*, and Eugene O'Neill released *The Hairy Ape;* and much earlier there had been several other serious protests. So Nathan reflects not only his own personal disenchantment, but also something of the general temper of his times. But because he mixes blame with sympathy, because he displaces living problems into the neutral realms of fantasy, and because he manages to suggest the longer perspectives of folkloristic story patterns, his criticism is usually gentler, his attitude more patient, than that of some of his contemporaries. To the popular writer, a quiet perseverance often seems more valid than the most rational rebellion.

The value of perseverance is apt to become even more apparent when the serious popular writer turns his attention from the relatively public and tangible problems of social processes to the more private and intangible ones of personal responsibility. In the case of *Autumn*—which not only denounces corruption in such public enterprises as business and education but deplores also the shrinking charity each private individual tends to exhibit to another in modern life—even the virtues of patience and love seem like radical correctives. The situation of John Wicket's lonely young widow poses such a private issue with blunt simplicity. John runs away from his parents' home in Barly, taking his father's money in the bargain; but he sees no reason to tell such sordid things to the girl he meets and marries. When his accidental death reveals he has a wife and baby, who are then brought back to live in Barly, village gossips thriftily shift their blame of dead John to his surviving widow. So the young woman becomes a target for sanctimonious bigots who systematically exclude her from all community affairs. A small, plain woman, inclined to shyness and silence, Widow Wicket finds her bereavement all the harder to bear because of this exclusion.

When at last another young man of the village begins to court her, however, his mother forces them to break off, whereupon the suitor enlists for the war and soon loses his life in France. The young woman is now doubly bereaved. But the grandmother of the dead soldier, driven by an unreasonable hostility, now charges the widow with driving her grandson to his untimely death. The whole community seems anxious to join in this ugly condemnation. In all of Barly, at any rate, only Mr. Jeminy really pities the young woman for her misfortune in marrying a thief, and senses the hope with which she must have considered a second marriage.

This blight in Barly warps every personal relationship. Except for Mr. Jeminy and young widow Wicket, each frail being in that countryside seems ready, even anxious, to judge and persecute any who may prove frailer than himself. The children too, for all their wide-eyed charm, betray a vicious want of simple charity. And Mr. Jeminy's housekeeper is frankly aghast when he proposes, in another community scandal, to adopt the infant of a village girl who bears a child out of wedlock. The housekeeper's private reasoning is thoroughly irresponsible and malignant: "There," she thinks to herself, "that's what comes to people like Mrs. Wicket" (140). But as a matter of fact there is no connection whatsoever between the misadventure of this second girl and the experience of the widow Wicket. One scapegoat serves all occasions. Even Margaret Bade, one of the kinder characters in the novel, is nevertheless like all women of that north country, "crabbed and twisted as their own apple trees" (171). Less in that spirit of Stoicism endorsed by Mr. Jeminy than in the blighted spirit of her own neighbors, Margaret Bade feels that life is "so much spilt milk" (169).

All in all, the fantasy in *Autumn,* although too often quaint or sentimental in detail, carries the most serious sort of implications. The novel can be read as a modern fable of material greed and spiritual malice, opposed by the single voice of the schoolmaster, whose meager force unfortunately cannot persuade an indifferent community that the problems he identifies are actually basic and endemic. A charming, sometimes humorous, often sentimental, barely plotted, and garrulous book, it is full of melodic prose and sententious argument, easily read, profoundly simple in the sense that all folk literature tends to be. Moreover, *Autumn* marks the beginning of Nathan's most characteristic work.

II *Fable on Strings*

The next short novel Nathan undertook to write was *The Puppet Master* (1923), where a more sophisticated variation on the folk theme that Carlo Lorenzini made famous fifty years before in *The Adventures of Pinocchio* is developed. Some measure of how deftly Nathan carried out his new project is suggested by the response the novel got from Vernon Louis Parrington, the sober critic of ideas in America, who called it the most graceful fantasy in American literature. Most of the reviewers, for that matter, were favorably impressed. Lloyd Morris, of the New York *Times*, thought it had the same poetic magic that had made *Autumn* such a distinguished work, and had other qualities also found in the best of James Barrie's work.

Donald Douglas, of the New York *Tribune*, took a slightly different tack. "Mr. Nathan is too genuine an artist for persons to call 'whimsical,' and unless he is very careful he will have to endure that word. No one wants to hear Mr. Nathan set down as 'reminiscent' of Barrie." Most of the reviews did agree, however, that in each new book Nathan published there was a growing precision and beauty of statement, a steadier vision of life embedded in the fabric of his imagination. "In one paragraph," said John Farrar in the course of his review of *The Puppet Master* for the *Bookman*, "Nathan says all that Floyd Dell really has to say about the younger generation."

What Nathan has to say in this 1923 novel about that younger generation is indeed more hopeful than most of his own previous observations had been. *Peter Kindred* ends on a bleak note, with the hero grimly preparing for a life of struggle and search. And *Autumn*, despite the frequent affirmations by Mr. Jeminy, leaves its readers with small reason to expect better things from any of the new generations of man. But *The Puppet Master*, for the first time, has a central character who seems genuinely optimistic about the future:

"Doctor Twine," said Papa Jonas solemnly, "you and I took over life as it was given us. We followed text, rules, manuals; and not our own hearts. I tell you that the young people to-day are following their hearts. They desire only to be honest, with others and with themselves. I like that, Dr. Twine; it does not make me comfortable, it often makes me anxious, but it fills me with hope. These young men and women are clearing the ground for those who come after. They are without respect, but that is because they have not found anything worthy of being respected. If in turn, they are not respected by those who come after them, that is their misfortune. At least those who follow will not be obliged to live an ugly life because they cannot help it. They will live as they think right. They will be free to love, because they will not have to ask any one's permission." (74-75)

The comment is probably too affirmative; it is both vague and oracular, and has no explicit function in the story. Precisely this kind of casual encouragement is often found in Nathan's work, for he is ever conscious of human fear and suffering and intends to offer comfort in his stories.

In *The Puppet Master* Nathan once again employs the rather static design in which a central observer, this time the old puppet master, Papa Jonas, patiently reflects on the tragi-comedy of events around him. In lieu of conventional plot, the novel gradually unfolds the basic complications of mortal love: the loss of childhood innocence that is typically involved, the ruthless propagation of the species which love insures, the fruitless effort of the partners to make each other over, the sacrificial nature of the marriage ceremony, the savagery of a loveless union, and much more. One part of the total pattern exhibits a child's sad compulsion to discover the kind of love that will inevitably terminate her simple trust and innocence; another presents a stark tragedy of love played out by fantastic surrogates, a rag doll and a wooden puppet; still another dramatizes an adult romance. Except for the story of the doll and puppet, which is a delightful mixture of moonshine and mayhem, animism and animalism, hope and helplessness, there is little dramtic action in the book.

Although there is a good deal of satire scattered throughout the story, touching on such subjects as institutional religion, celibacy for philosophers, and the strange compulsions generated by love, Nathan's ridicule is always tempered with sympathy; there are moments of absolute farce, savage realism, unrestrained sentimentality, and exquisite irony; but they are all imbedded in a timeless patience. The book abounds in laughter, yet the final impression is that engendered by a sad melodrama.

III   *A Biblical Fable*

Robert Nathan was born on January 2, 1894, to Harold Nathan and Sarah (Gruntal) Nathan. He is a direct descendant of Rabbi Gersham Seixas, one of the incorporators of Columbia College in the eighteenth century. Although Nathan came from a distinguished family, which included rabbis and secular leaders in the Jewish community of America, he broke away from this pattern:

As a child, I was brought up in the liberal, the reformed faith. When I was very young, my mother wanted me to be a rabbi. But something must have gone wrong—for in my earliest memories the child I was found it almost impossible to distinguish between Judaism and Christianity. I never thought of myself as a Christian, but I experienced the same feeling of love and wonder from God's relation to Jesus as I did from His relation to Moses and Elijah. It didn't seem strange to me that Jesus was God's son; for I thought that we were all of us God's sons. As a boy I went to the old Temple Emanuel; at school in New England I went to the Congregational Church; the temple service seemed more beautiful to me, but the spirit of the church was kinder. I said my prayers every night until I was well through college, but I was never able to think of God as a Jew or a Christian; He was just God, everybody's God.[2]

As Nathan grew older and read more widely, he came to recognize that God, at least within the terms of his own experience, was many different Gods—Catholic, Jew, Episcopalian, Moslem, Baptist, Mormon. The Deity, in fact, was different in each of these representations—in aim and sympathy, as well as in point of view. "And all those different people who were God seemed to be busy making little heavens for themselves, and little hells for everybody else. So I grew sceptical of that God who was so many different people."[2]

Nathan published these biographical remarks in 1933, but the essential aspects of his personal conviction could have been inferred from the fiction he published earlier. In the semi-autobiographical *Peter Kindred,* for example, such a gradual alienation is also presented, culminating in the stark fictional scene in which a bereaved father, his head bowed over shivering hands, yearns desperately for a power in control, a power he can hate, some wise impersonal force. In *Autumn* a frankly jaundiced view of conventional religions is found in the schoolmaster's blunt speech at Mrs. Grumble's deathbed; " 'You God,' " Mr. Jeminy says then, " 'this is your doing. Then come and be present; receive the forgiveness of this good woman, to whom you gave, in this life, poverty and sacrifice' " (194). In *The Puppet Master* this hint of outrage gives way to good-natured scepticism. Sectarian claims are refuted not by argument, but by a rabbit's escapade. Modern faith, according to Papa Jonas, needs the exhilaration of a fresh burning of heretics. And there is a tendency in that novel to pay homage to pagan principles which still lie beneath the surface of more recent religious practice.

But the essential nature of God did not become a central theme in Nathan's fiction until he wrote *Jonah* (1925). This novel, however, is anything but a solemn ontological inquiry. The story is simply a fictional elaboration of the famous prophecy set forth in the Old Testament. There is no pretense at serious exegesis, and yet the story is indeed concerned about the nature of God—and the nature of His creature, man. In both style and format this fresh telling of the impudence of Jonah is an advance over the previous novels; the prose is lyrical but crisp, and the design is clear and tight.

Anatole France provided some inspiration. "In those days," runs the opening sentence of *Thaïs* (1890), "the desert was peopled with anchorites." On this prophetic note the French author begins his secular account of a saint's mortal and immortal adventures. Beneath an ingenious brocade of often irreverent comment, the action of his novel demonstrates that even holy undertakings may be confused in motive, distracted by instinct, plagued with false starts, doubts, and disappointments. And so utterly human did Anatole France make both his saintly man and his worldly courtesan that a reversal in their respective roles seems wholly credible and deliciously ironic.

"In those days," reads the opening sentence of *Jonah*, "there were prophets in the land." Nathan too catches the awesome lilt of ritual language as he begins his story of the private life and personal frustrations of the prophet Jonah. Even more sympathetically then Anatole France, whose novel is riddled with scepticism and higher learning, Nathan demonstrates how quickly human love can distract divine ambition, how petty regimens may paralyze respected institutions, how all mortal notions of God tend to be ridiculous, and why fumbling, wrong-headed humanity is a natural object for satire and affection; for, where Anatole France bedazzles reason, Nathan simply convinces the heart. Though the story of *Jonah* is presented in the unheroic terms of ordinary life, it is based directly on the biblical account and is concerned with the central burden of that older prophecy: the nature and dominion of God as revealed by the fortuitous rebellion of a prophet. But always the real sympathy of Nathan is with man in his human condition.

If the tone and exposition of *Jonah* evoke sympathy, the protagonist himself generates tension. Gone from this book is the passive interlocutor of the Barly stories, the gentle sage who ruminates on human folly with patience, wit, and charity, but who seldom acts with much effect. Young Jonah is an active, impatient, hopeful, willful human being whose every action helps define the central meaning of the novel.

Beginning in a naïve faith that his own particular notion of God is wholly sufficient, and encouraged in his faith by the new attention his initial auguries have brought him from those who benefit by them, Jonah is obviously cut from a very human pattern. One day when he falls in love, as even young prophets do, his first impulse is to find some way to reconcile his spiritual dedication and his new worldly desires. Finding this reconciliation impossible, but driven still by love, Jonah decides to give up the accolades of prophecy for a more prosaic but connubial life. Even then, with scruples put aside, there is still the problem of supporting a prospective family. He attempts to convert his prophetic reputation into a church appointment, or into some civic post; but he discovers that a liaison with God qualifies him for no sinecures on earth. Without worldly means he is, of course, obliged to give up worldly ambitions. His beloved promptly takes another for her lover.

Jonah's only recourse is to return to the desert where he had first won fame. Then God demands that he go to cry out against the wicked city of Nineveh. Jonah promptly objects. In Nathan's book the young man's reaction is justified by human considerations: " 'Oh,' he cried bitterly, all the passion in his heart storming out at last in a torrent of despair, 'You . . . what are You God of? Were You God of Israel when a Tyrian stole my love? Was I Your prophet then?' " (183).

Although Nathan does create this pattern of personal motivation out of whole cloth, he is careful to present the conventional theme with a minimum of distortion. Jonah's old teacher, Naaman, lectures his protégé on the fallacy of thinking that God is no more than a local deity; and on more than one occasion in the novel God himself protests at parochialism in Israel, saying for example: " 'It is your fault, Moses, that the Jews believe I belong to them entirely. Well, I don't blame you, for you could not have brought them safely through the desert otherwise' " (170). But however circumspect he is in major principles, Nathan is more than ready to extrapolate details. *Jonah* shows that not only men, but creatures of every kind, suffer the common illusions about God. In the fantasy of the novel—which has some precedent, after all, in the fantasy of the Bible—there is a desert fox who is convinced God must be a jackal until one day a jackal eats his wife; thereupon the fox, bemused as ever, decides God must really be a raven. With the same myopia, actually, the whale prefers to think that even if God may have many images He can most naturally be conceived as a whale.

This willful tendency in man to cherish misconceptions has drastic consequences: in failing to comprehend the majesty and mystery of God, man proves he has not yet recognized the miracle of earth itself, even though it is everywhere defined in beauty. Nathan offers in evidence a beetle with a bright green coat soberly walking toward his house: "Presently an ant approached him and gave him a bite on the leg. The beetle turned an anxious look on his tiny assailant, whose head barely came up to his knee, 'Come, come,' he exclaimed, 'have you no respect for beauty? Do you think God enjoys having you bite me? He would be much upset if anything happened to me'" (52). Whether this be argument reduced to the absurd, or truth exposed by absurd argument, it is typical of Nathan.

While modern readers may feel amused by the narrow, literal, and plural views of God that men once held in Israel, Jonah, who is of that age, has yet to learn about such things as monotheism. So the rebel Jonah—having fled what he takes to be the jurisdiction of Iaveh, only to be trapped by a storm at sea with shipmates who feel they can survive only by placating the God of the Jews—is of course cast overboard and caught up by the whale. In the process he learns the orthodox lesson that God is everywhere; He commands the fish of the sea, the hosts of the air, and the creatures on land. However, the lesson which the author of the novel proposes—the idea that love of earth is holy—has not been mastered by the still embittered young man. In a subsequent episode, for example, when a green beetle crosses his path, the stiff-necked Jonah goes a few steps out of his way to tread upon it.

Despite Jonah's persistent tendency to express his personal rebellion, he seems ready at last to execute the mission to Nineveh; and he does go to cry out against that wicked city, expecting to see the foreigners chastised by his omnipotent God. When they repent and therefore win mercy, Jonah is again irate. Then the vine is made to grow and to die, as God explains that infinite power includes infinite mercy. This is of course the conventional theological message of the Book of Jonah.

Nathan's novel then shows that Jonah is still too arrogant to acquiesce in this large conception of deity. As a matter of fact, the author explains, he really "was not a prophet; he was a man, like anybody else, whose love had been false, whose God had been unkind" (211). Even the Lord expresses disappointment in the young man, who has simply been a patriot and who is still blind to universal beauty: "He is convinced that I am God of Israel alone. I do not mind that point of view in a prophet, but it will not do in a poet. Severity, glory, knowledge, belong to the nations, if you like. But beauty belongs to the world. It is the portion of all mankind in its God" (169-70).

Not only does Nathan's extrapolation of the original prophecy attempt to explain the personal motives and behavior of young Jonah, but it also suggests that his obdurate behavior is characteristic of the chosen people: "High among the clouds, God turned sadly to Moses. 'You Jews,' He said wearily, 'you do not understand beauty. With you it is either glory or despair'" (211-12). This obviously is no blind indictment of Jews, though it does illustrate a common capacity among Jewish writers to be critical of their own habits and traditions; and, as in Nathan's case, it implies a confidence that their behavior and ideals can survive responsible criticism. In *Jonah,* and elsewhere in his work, Nathan presents the Jews as very ordinary human beings who have their normal quota of heroes, saints, fools, scoundrels, and men of destiny. His terminal emphasis in this novel simply points up the generally recognized distinction between the Jews, who seem to seek their fulfillment solemnly because of their profound and often mirthless sense of duty, and the Greeks, who seemingly seek their fulfillment in a flair of joy and beauty because of their persistent curiosity. The contrast offers a fitting conclusion to Nathan's study of a representative Jewish man.

IV   *Fabliaux Picaresque*

Although separated from *Autumn* by some five years in terms of composition and by three intervening publications, *The Fiddler in Barly* (1926) is actually a continuation of the pastoral design introduced in that earlier book. A new cast has been recruited in order to dramatize another aspect of the general situation which both books treat, but the literary technique is much the same. Once again the author employs a mature man as the central figure in his story—another sanely modest, common-flavored, soothsaying kind of man whom he thinks qualified to serve as chorus for the sad old comedy of life that never ends. In *Autumn* the role is vested in Mr. Jeminy, the patiently resigned old schoolmaster whose gentle censure of utilitarian education comprises the major argument of a book almost devoid of customary action. In *The Fiddler in Barly* the central role is vested in a strolling musician of sorts, a rustic apologist for art and simple joys, who plays a fiddle while his dog dances for coins. This fiddler, Lindeman, like the schoolmaster of *Autumn,* has an honest love for the homely splendors of earth and a deep sympathy for people. But he is far more aggressive than Mr. Jeminy, and therefore more interesting to readers who enjoy at least a modicum of conflict and plot in their fiction.

The same bleak social contagion still hangs over Barly, where a Reverend Flood grimly instructs his flock about the importance of being sober and penitent. Village gossips have discovered fresh cause for trouble in the dancing of a child called Metabel, whose happiness vexes them. And the young Edna Flood feels cold and dark with shame when she succumbs to a lover; she is grateful that she does not enjoy love since she is convinced such behavior should wait "until they were married, and then only in the dark, and she'd close her eyes. It was her duty then, and so she'd do it" (151). In Barly, obviously, piety is conceived as penance, propriety as persecution, and indecorous love as lust.

Although the fiddler is more charitable in judging human behavior than his neighbors are, and does much to discredit the "blue-nosed" customs of the village, first by contradicting the joyless Reverend Flood at every opportunity, and next by setting an example of *joie de vivre* himself, it is actually the subhuman menagerie in the book who provide the best parody of human behavior. Mrs. Sebold's hens, like village housewives everywhere, are always "anxious to be second rather than first" and so rush ahead of one another, only to wait for the others to catch up again (14-15). A bull cricket, on the other hand, exhibits a masculine impatience with the notion of waiting. Upon being questioned about his casual intercourse with a passing female cricket, he responds with a hearty self-assurance. " 'Yes,' he said, 'it is love.' And he added stoutly a moment later, 'I believe in love. But I do not believe in talking about it a great deal. No: with me it is jump first, and then conversation' " (47).

Love is naturally an important topic in a novel so much concerned with the joys of living. On this topic the fiddler's dog, Musket, considers himself a connoisseur. He is frank enough to admit that as an artist, a dancer, he has certain opportunities; still he feels that falling in love with a friend always proves better than flirting with strangers. He speaks of course with the *savoir-faire* of the confirmed bachelor.

Not all males can speak from Musket's experience, but this seldom causes them to do so with less assurance. The rooster Bartholomew—for love, he hopes, if not for glory—is bumptious enough to turn fighting cock even though he has no ring experience of any kind: " 'I am in fine shape,' he said; 'I am very confident, and feel sure that I will soon peck the other bird to pieces. I have one blow which starts from the ground, and is apt to destroy anything. Would you like to see it?' " (164-65).

But, if males tend to arrogance, are females tender and selfless? Nathan offers another parable in parody about a charming canary who wants to be a great singer. She falls in love with a handsome mocking bird who, in the hope she will then fly off to make a new home with him, patiently teaches her all he knows. At the last moment, however, she finds it impossible to leave her bathtub, her apple, and her art; and he goes off alone and is eaten by hawks on his homeward journey. Upon learning of his fate, the canary expresses her honest concern: " 'See what would have happened to me if I had married him?' " (53).

In contrast with the customary norms of satire, such gentle mockery seems delicate and unconvincing; for it offers criticism without demanding a serious reaction or commitment. Nathan favors passages in which the humor is supposed to play diminuendo, and he has a habit, especially in his early fantasies, of using coy little creatures or such lovable large ones to represent man's follies that censure is forgotten. In such bland fantasy the sophisticated reader finds little cause for empathy. In *The Fiddler in Barly* these small creatures serve, however, a useful function. When Nathan addresses the public issues of his story, he usually employs human characters such as Lindeman to contradict sterile dogma or to expose bigotry; but, when he appeals to the

[46]

private conscience of his reader, Nathan typically employs the demi-spirits of fantasy to enact the covert drama of common human failings.

In *The Woodcutter's House* (1927), a sequel to *The Fiddler in Barly*, we get some inkling of how much Nathan himself enjoyed the mockery in miniature of his previous novel. He keeps as leading figures in the new story not only the girl Metabel, now sixteen, but also the aging but still amorous Musket. In terms of dramatic focus the dog's adventures provide, in fact, the richest comedy in the book.

Since Musket's previous appearance in the earlier novel he has grown so sophisticated that he now appears as the canine model of a worldly, sated, bachelor rogue. Against his wit, experience, and winning ways no member of the gentler sex appears to have much chance. It is small wonder that a mouse seeks his advice about an unchaste female whom he nevertheless adores. Musket is more than ready to give advice. Women, he explains, are unfaithful by instinct, inclination, and the force of circumstances; but he finally advises the mouse to marry. However, like most who give advice, Musket intends it for someone else. When a new dog called Susan one day appears in town, he makes it clear that no coquette will ever snare him; but, when he notices the growing company that attends her, that resolve is strangely shaken. Soon each of them makes elaborate plans to meet the other as though by accident; and, when that meeting does occur, it blooms with mutual interest, spiced with antagonism, which leads to an unhappy separation and then to a fervent reconciliation. Musket archly suggests a stroll in the woods, to which Susan demurely consents. The stage is set for the defeat of the undefeatable:

> Heavy heat lay on the hillside that afternoon, heat almost as heavy as a mist. The birds were still, even the crows forgot to caw; only a locust stung the silence with the drill of his sound. At the wood's edge Metabel came upon Musket; the little dog's head was hanging, and he dragged his feet wearily. Susan walked beside him; she took mincing steps, and gazed at him in a hopeful way. But Musket did not return her glances. When he passed Metabel, he hung his head lower than ever. Finally his legs collapsed, and he sat down. "Ak," he said. "Yoo. My legs are not what they used to be."
>
> Susan wished to console him. "Never mind," she said; "I

am not sad about this, really. Supposing that in the future we simple confine ourselves to conversation? Come, cheer up; life is not all what-you-may-call-it." (147-48)

Although politely phrased, and broken into incidents scattered through both the novels which deal with Musket, the basic story elements correspond to those which characterize a medieval fabliau—a rapid sequence of events forms a single episode; the humor of the situation has its roots in human nature; and "the cream of the jest" involves humiliation of the male by a female's sex intrigue. Although this fabliau in fantasy is not actually the major story line—which is concerned with the human events of Metabel's visit to a pristine valley where a young man threatens to destroy the ancient trees he worships because of his new love for Metabel—the comedy acted out by hens, roosters, crickets, mouse, robin, horse, and dogs is the best part of the book; for it manages to reduce all human pretension to genial absurdity.

Both in *The Fiddler in Barly* and in *The Woodcutter's House* Nathan employs fantasy not only to achieve the displacement necessary to his satire—reducing the complex urban problems to rural simplicity in order to magnify the greed, malice, and folly involved in modern life—but also to create a *double-entendre* within the story itself. Thus an adult, humorously candid, but seldom brutal, and never simply prurient pattern of meaning evolves from the creatures of fantasy; and this pattern tends to offset and balance the rather moody prose, mystical gravity, and melodramatic pattern of human affairs.

V   Character Types

Not that Nathan's human characters are without interest of their own; at least three basic character types can be identified. First, there is the archetypal figure of the secular rabbi, the dedicated leader whose authority has been diminished by gradual erosion of the tradition for which he speaks and whose own convictions often derive from worldly philosophies which supplement, even when they do not supplant, the older doctrines of his religion. In *Jewish Wit* Theodor Reik reminds us that the rabbi today is very often a pathetic or comic figure of Jewish folk humor. Certainly Mr. Jeminy, the earnest schoolmaster in *Autumn*, while he is indeed patterned on a Catholic saint, does spend his life in a Puritanical community, and is most often an apologist for Stoicism, does behave very like a secular rabbi bent on saving his fellows from their own corruption and folly.

A second character type developed in these early books is the man in search of his identity. Peter Kindred anticipates the lonely, doubtful, but desperately hopeful sort of sceptic found in several of Nathan's novels; but Peter does not fully comprehend the awesome ambiguity of his own mortality since he still assumes that finding God will solve the mystery of his personal existence. The young prophet Jonah illustrates a still deeper sense of human insecurity; for, while he recognizes God, he still cannot believe that man counts for so little within the scheme of omnipotence. What then is man, such a doubtful character is apt to ask; and who are the Chosen People since they must endure the agony of His grace?

A third character type is the Shlemihl, a comic variant of the serious doubter. The perennial bad luck of this Jewish folk figure is usually understood to spring from his own ineptitude, from the cosmic joke of man's grand ambition and pitiful performance.[3] Mr. Lindeman, the fiddler who nobly contends against bigotry in *Barly*, is nevertheless capable of confounding any situation when he tries to help. Given money to buy a dress for an injured child, Lindeman bets it impulsively on a cockfight, only to lose it all when the cocks themselves refuse to fight to the finish. This sort of joke is precisely the type found in many Jewish proverbs in which the Shlemihl, born to lose but also a willing agent in his own defeat, kills a chicken only to have it walk, winds a clock only to have it stop, or falls on his back only to break his nose.

Obviously Nathan's characterization owes a good deal to the popular conceptions of man defined by Jewish folklore. His early books, at least, are well populated by men who think and act like secular rabbis, who anxiously search for identity and God, and who often betray their human frailty in conduct expected of a Shlemihl.

VI *Conservative Aspects of Popular Tradition*

The very themes of Nathan's early books are those we might expect a secular rabbi to treat, and the treatment they receive reflects the conservative temper of popular tradition.

It is true that Edith McEwen Dorian, writing in the troubled context of the 1933 economic disaster, could be most impressed by Nathan's apparent interest in reform. "Like others of the younger American intellectuals whose work began to make itself felt in the nineteen twenties," she says, "Nathan has been concerned for a civilization subservient to the materialistic ideals of the machine age. He has shown scant sympathy for the destruction of beauty at the dictates of the acquisitive instinct. He has shown even less for the representative forms of a middle class Puritanism only half-alive but still warping the hard mind and negating tolerance."[4] So far as she goes, Dorian is correct.

In *Autumn*, Nathan satirizes materialism and bigotry; in *The Puppet Master*, he twits church dogmatists, grieves for the artist trapped in a cash-and-carry-world, and complains about female domination in modern life; in *Jonah*, he shows how an obsession with literal meanings can destroy the poetic instinct, how formal systems can strangle natural faith, and how arrogance can drive man into the prison of himself; in *The Fiddler in Barly*, he ridicules the joyless world of a dead orthodoxy that fosters social injustice; and, in *The Woodcutter's House*, he dramatizes the joy and humor in our condition while emphasizing the awful loss men always suffer when in their greed they destroy the primitive beauty of nature.

But Nathan's criticism, typically oblique, is muted by the esthetic distance created by his fantasy; folly and fraud seem to be tolerated by the patience of his sad exposition, and half-excused by his painful laughter. In contrast to the militant assault of Naturalistic writers or to the ruthless scorn of the *avant garde*, his mellow lament upon the state of society seems too temperate. But most popular writers are deeply conservative. As Walter Fuller Taylor explains in *The Economic Novel in America*, Mark Twain strenuously denounced industrial corruption in his society, yet all he really wanted was reasonable control of obvious abuses, for he desired no change in familiar patterns. And as Mark Schorer concludes in *Sinclair Lewis*, that satirist also settled happily for the stolidity in American life he most often castigated in fiction. Upon reflection it seems safe to say that most popular writers are especially conscious of the inertia in human affairs, of the conservative instincts which survive from generation to generation, of the cumulative meaning in our social customs, perhaps because it is the ground on which they meet a general audience.

Nathan's patience has even deeper resonances; in addition to the democratic overtones of the American consensus in which he lived, there are undertones which must have persisted through millennia of Jewish experience. By keeping this older range of conventional feeling always in mind, we may even come to understand the sentimentality in his work. For there is indeed an almost blatant sentimentality in many of Nathan's early books, as in *Autumn* where the schoolmaster reduces the precedent of Saint Francis to a dainty self-pity by asking if the trees, meadows, and little paths have not enjoyed the daisy chains his pupils have been wont to make (144); in *The Puppet Master* where a delightful parody of Christian Science dissolves at last into pure schmaltz (196-97); in *The Fiddler in Barly* where the narrator intrudes upon the story of Metabel to warn against the inevitable course of events, thus begging his dramatic case as shamelessly as Barrie ever did for Tinkerbell (140). And it is not enough to explain that Nathan counted on his reader to understand the humor which is also involved in his hyperbole.

Irving Howe argues,[5] at any rate, that, while sentimentality is indeed a common weakness of much Jewish writing, the employment of this tone may not be quite so fatal as some modern critics think. For the emotional attitudes and ideological convictions at the base of one particular culture, Howe says, may differ radically from those which underlie a second culture; and what seems to be an emotion in excess of the occasion within the first context may seem, nevertheless, altogether proper within the second. A desperate reliance upon composure, often reflected in the modern cult of understatement, and justified by the assumption that it is good to feel but bad to show feeling—however common such a theory and practice may be in Anglo-American literature—may seem quite as alien and therefore false to readers who are Jewish, French, or Italian as their Mediterranean temperaments must seem to readers who are not accustomed to ready tears and demonstrative behavior.

Nathan, who is entirely conscious of the greater range of emotional expression that Jewish culture permits, is often tempted to write as though his readers all were conscious of it too. But even a popular writer suffers if he permits sentiment to burgeon into sentimentality, and in later works Nathan tends to be more restrained.

For the most part, however, Nathan's imaginative use of broad popular traditions in his early fantasies is effective. The literary forms that he adapts from the parables of Saint Francis, from various folktales past and present and from ancient modes of oral humor and biblical prophecy are the natural literary definitions of the conventional wisdom he examines and endorses. Language and situation are consistently simple, the biblical imagery derives of course from the commonest book in Western culture, his characters are usually traditional types we often find in folklore, and his fundamental appeal is to our deepest feelings and instincts. In his early work, certainly, Nathan seems indeed to speak most often in the conservative voice of popular tradition.

CHAPTER 3

The Sound of Time Retreating in the Dark

I N THE mellow retrospect that Nathan presents in *The Wilderness Stone* (1961), the early years of the twentieth century seem gay and golden, a time when the air was full of promise and the news was always good. Had not Admiral Robert Peary recently conquered the Pole? Was not Charles Lindbergh ready to fly the Atlantic? Was not George Gershwin about to write *Rhapsody in Blue?* For any young man living in the 1920's the whole world, according to Nathan's semi-autobiographical novel, must have seemed brave and new. "Of course," the author admits, "we had our bad times too. But even in the bad times, in the crash and the Depression, the broken lives, the suicides, the hungry, homeless men and worn-down women, with dust covering the heroes, covering the farms and ranges of the Panhandle, covering the *Rhapsody in Blue*—even then there was something, almost a gaiety, bitter as gall, perhaps, and grim, but brotherly" (54).

But this nostalgic story of those early years tends to gloss over the private inner tensions Nathan sometimes felt. There is scarcely any hint in *The Wilderness Stone,* for example, of the estrangement he endured simply because he chose to be a writer. His immediate family offered encouragement, to be sure, even though his mother once cherished hope that he might become a rabbi; and other professional writers judged him simply as a person and by the things he published. But in the social community, beyond his family and exclusive of the writing fraternity, Nathan was measured by the usual, American materialistic standards. "I was the one," he said years later, "who did not become a doctor, or lawyer, or stockbroker, or businessman—and make a lot of money, marry, have children, and live in a big house."

When the Depression came, however, the status problems of

one young writer were quite overwhelmed by the survival problems of society at large. The family, which had seemed such a bastion to Nathan in his younger days, was itself now threatened; and the pervasive fear he saw on every hand jolted Nathan out of his customary abstract themes and remote settings. Some of his best-loved stories reflect his fresh sympathy for people caught in the ordinary frustrations of these years of turmoil. But his fiction is less inclined to challenge fate than to comfort those who cannot escape it, and the novels he wrote in the later 1920's and in the 1930's are still characterized by a pastoral point of view and by melodramatic resolutions.

I   Urban Pastorals

Except for *The Puppet Master*, all of Nathan's early fantasies have rural settings; and they rely on nostalgic mood, traditional arguments, and folkloristic characters and situations. With only one exception his next eight novels employ some urban setting or metropolitan frame of reference, but they do so chiefly to suggest modern decadence. The deliberate contrast of gross present circumstances and the memory of some idyllic past results in fantasies best described as urban pastorals.

The Bishop's Wife (1928) is an allegorical fantasy in which the unhappy, sterile, unfeeling materialism of modern urban life is contrasted to an all but forgotten conception of Edenic bliss. The bishop of the story has only the vestigial interests which pass today for religious concern. He is chiefly concerned not with love and charity but with controlling two cathedrals; twenty churches; twelve parish houses; two deans; three archdeacons; more than one hundred curates, deacons, and sextons; seven female auxiliaries; and a great deal of money. His greatest aspiration is to build still another cathedral, and his most pressing need is for an archdeacon with a "good hand at figures, a tongue of fire in the pulpit, a healing way with the doubtful, a keen eye for the newspapers" (3).

All the same, when an angel who identifies himself as Michael suddenly appears to fill this vacancy on the church staff, the bishop soon begins to think he is receiving more help than he bargained for. Not that Michael is less than masterful in all the business transactions he undertakes, but he is a masculine spirit and so reacts with honest gusto to all the suppressed charms of the bishop's wife. Michael's angelic proposition is the ironic climax of the story, for it requires that the bishop's wife choose between a loveless, routine, inhibited mode of modern life with her husband, and a momentary surrender to the raptures of heavenly love. As usual in a Nathan story, the situation rather than the resolution is of greatest interest; that the bishop's wife resists temptation in the end is not what we are most apt to remember.

If the city of man has indeed grown so stale, weary, and unprofitable that even the primeval temptation has lost its charm, can mankind still hope for better things in the City of God? *There Is Another Heaven* (1929) examines the future life that the Anglo-Saxon Protestant majority presumably expects to find in such a city on the other side of Jordan. A character called Wutheridge, once professor of Semitic languages before he arrived in that particular heaven, tries to explain the nature of the place to a man who arrives still later—a Mr. Lewis, born Levi, who has forsaken his own ancestral faith in the hope of finding Jesus there in what he thinks is His heaven. Wutheridge can offer him no encouragement:

> "No, my friend," he remarked, sinking back again, "this is a city made to receive in beatitude those who have gone regularly to church, and have not sinned too much. Its citizenry numbers many important people, but not the great archangels of the Thebaid, the Kerubs of Safed, or the Saints of Rome; and not, so far as I know, that most mystic of all figures, Jesus, the Son of Man.
>
> "However, I do not see why it should trouble you."
>
> "Trouble me," groaned Mr. Lewis.
>
> "Unless," continued the professor, "you care for theology in other than a practical sense."
>
> And he looked earnestly and sympathetically at Mr. Lewis, who nodded his head sadly.
>
> "I guess that's it," he said. "I was born to it."
>
> "Of course," agreed the professor enthusiastically: "I had forgotten that you belong to the race of psalmists, of the prophets, of Hillel of Jerusalem, of Philo of Alexandria, of Loria of Safed, of Jochai, of Akiba, of Eliezer of Worms. Now you find yourself among such men as Oliver Cromwell and W. J. Bryan. Well, that is sad for you."

And placing his hand on Mr. Lewis' knee, he inquired anxiously,
"Why did you do it?" (114-15)

Why indeed? But then Lewis, born Levi, is not the only one to mistake a sterile conventionality for spiritual meaning. Except for Wutheridge, Lewis, and one artless youngster, all the characters Nathan uses to people his mock-heaven are pious frauds without the wit to recognize their own self-deception. There are, for example, the familiar female activist who postures like a saint but who is engrossed in promoting mundane causes; a gaggle of eternal adolescents who romp about with animal vigor and heavenly abandon; various unconfessed bigots who take shelter in the hollow sanctity of ugly custom; and an administrative churchman who indulges his old compulsions to engage in paper work and politics. On every side we find nothing but transplanted follies from a materialistic, urban, spiritless existence. Small wonder, then, that Wutheridge, Lewis, and the child are disenchanted by the celestial company they find and so decide to flee to some other heaven.

In *The Orchid* (1931) the city once again provides a sinister frame of reference for a fable of pastoral simplicity. Mrs. Alma Heavenstreet has let herself get so engrossed in the routines of a meaningless, metropolitan existence that she is no longer important to her husband, who for his part has so far succumbed to Manhattan madness that he hopes to buy the permanent affection of a glamorous actress and live in ecstasy with her abroad. But that actress has also been schooled in city ways, knows what it means to surrender her position as the toast of the town, and shrewdly anticipates that the paramour of a wealthy but fickle businessman may have a chancy future.

The situation takes on a comic aspect when befuddled Mrs. Heavenstreet gets her errant husband to take her to the theater in the secret hope that she can learn from this very actress, whom she does not suspect of anything, enough worldly wiles to win her husband back. But the cheap surface pattern takes on new meaning when Mrs. Heavenstreet accidentally discovers their affair. She does not react in anger, and she does not spend pity on herself. Instead, she recognizes how frail the average marriage is, being a union of simply mortal creatures; how pitiable her husband really is in his lugubrious infidelity; and how much she herself is responsible for keeping their love vital. That the actress finally elects to continue with her stage career, that Mrs. Heavenstreet recaptures the interest of her husband by means of homely artifice, and that the whole story terminates in happy farce is relatively unimportant. The simple sanctity of old-fashioned marriage has triumphed over all the distractions and corruptions of modern sophistication.

In *Winter in April* (1937)—also set in New York, a city deceptively beautiful by day but obviously sinister at night—fifteen-year-old Ellen suffers for the first time from the common scourge of unrequited love. Her awkwardly ingenuous behavior in the presence of Eric von Siegenfels, a European refugee for whose attention she tries to compete with a sophisticated woman of the world, and her silent sacrifice when that young man finally decides to return to Europe to fight for his homeland are typical of her idyllic tragedy—the young girl struggling to escape from the innocence of childhood only to discover that love, far from providing the freedom of which she dreams, is simply the initiation into new adult obligations. To anyone who has read two or three of Nathan's novels both this theme and the situation are familiar. But all of Nathan's work, perhaps because it is influenced by the method and meaning of the Psalms, is rich in repeated themes, recurrent imagery, familiar character types, and archetypal situations that differ only superficially from book to book.

Winter in April, though modern and fairly realistic, has much the same perspective as the other urban pastorals. Henry Pennifer, for example, who is described as a critic of letters, member of the American Academy of Arts and Letters, editor emeritus of the *University Quarterly*, and winner of last year's Pulitzer prize, is certainly an interesting character in his own right. He has little sympathy for writers who are obliged, as he says, to tuck themselves away in cotton-wool in order to write; for he thinks a writer should make his own peace around him and get on with his work (63). He also thinks it odd that we are proud of our poets only after they are dead, and honor instead the critics who write books about them (95); he professes to stand in awe of popular writers who make so much money and sell their stories to motion picture companies, and yet he cannot read their books (128); he finds, indeed, that many modern novels seem to begin at the bottom and then go down (22). He recognizes that the spirit of this age is to be tough (11); and he concedes that man is the cruellest and the most implacable enemy of man, but feels that one day man may master his own passion for destruction—a thought which, incidentally, makes Pennifer appear to be a sentimentalist to his contemporaries (166).

And yet Pennifer, despite his ability to understand himself and his modern world, more often thinks and speaks in the traditional manner of the narrators in Nathan's earlier books. He too knows, for instance, about the strange despair of youth (5), nourishes the old hope that love is eternal (86), thinks marriage may indeed be a form of immolation (26), and in the very mystery of existence finds evidence for belief in God (7). Mr. Jeminy; the Puppet Master; Jonah's mentor; the fiddler Lindeman; and the narrator in later novels could all subscribe without reservation to these same hopes and beliefs.

This obvious repetition in theme and treatment has contradictory implications. On the one hand, it suggests how often Nathan uses fictional characters as spokesmen for his personal point of view; only an omniscient author could achieve such unanimity among so many different narrators in so many different books. On the other hand, it also illustrates how often an older and essentially impersonal mode of story-telling influences his work; for Nathan is one of a disappearing breed, an author fully conscious of the popular tradition conveyed by oral literature in the past, a story-teller more intent upon preserving the wisdom of the race in tales of wonder and common sense than in inventing some novelty of his own.

Some reviewers, to be sure, think such repetition simply demonstrates the author's limited power of invention. There is justice in the charge, but not so much as casual critics like to suppose. *Winter in April* and the other urban pastorals, while they do not represent a major literary invention, are nevertheless unique adaptations of ancient imaginative modes to contemporary circumstances. These novels blend Jewish wit and Romantic nostalgia, satirical entertainment and folk wisdom, biblical rhythm and repetend with the idioms of ordinary modern life. And they do so to create a popular affirmation of the possibilities for meaningful life in spite of the threats and tensions of materialistic, urban, corporate, and spiritless circumstances which characterize our time.

II *Stories of Symbolic Escape*

The basic paradox upon which the urban pastorals depend—lost modern man's stubborn refusal to be guided by tradition—recurs quite often in Nathan's fiction. As we have seen, it can be the source of comic and pathetic insights, the grounds for common sympathy and familiar argument; but it can also foster a mood of quiet desperation in readers who assent to the author's interpretation. Nathan himself falls victim to this mood from time to time, as he does in verse that sometimes darkly broods upon the sound of time retreating in the dark.[1] But in fiction his primary objective is to offer entertainment, confirmation, and consolation, rather than to insist upon the terror and suffering in human experience. Because of this intent he often includes some sort of melodramatic resolution in his stories.

One More Spring (1933) was written at a time when Americans were all but panic-stricken by wholesale unemployment, farm and business foreclosures, bank failures, hunger marches, and by the fear of fear itself. Disillusioned and frustrated, the mass of people sought some escape in fantasy; as a consequence, this era was the heyday of formula magazine fiction, radio soap opera, motion picture melodrama, and costume novels. But the Americans who consumed this fare also wanted reassurance—not merely that prosperity was "just around the corner," as the songs and slogans claimed, but that the old truths their fathers held to be self-evident would still provide America with the resolution to carry on. Because it catered to such current needs it is small wonder that Nathan's novel about the Great Depression became his first popular success.

One More Spring is a fantasy about the "forgotten man," a generic term for all the dispossessed; he was once expected to be the master of the New World, the democratic hero of the American myth. But Jared Otkar, whose little antique shop in New York simply fails, is presented as the victim of economic attitudes and forces that leave him homeless and bewildered: "For the old faiths were gone, and he had nothing to put in their places. That innocence of mind with which, in the past, men had clung to their beliefs, no longer existed in this world. In the midst of the most dreadful disasters, they had perished happily for the sake of God, for the East India Company, science, the divine right of kings, or the dawn of democracy. Now they were obliged to die for no other reason than starvation" (8-9).

Nathan chooses to tell his story from a sadly comic point of view, in which the actual pain and blank frustration of the time are often muted. Even the suicide attempt of a distraught banker is reduced to farce. The episode does point up the human weakness of the Wall Street oligarch and includes wry jokes about financial expedients, but there is no rancor in the exposition. True enough, the episode is not logical; but neither is the major action of the book, which brings together merchant, strumpet, fiddler, and banker who sleep together in one huge antique bed during a fugitive winter in Central Park. Indeed, what passes for logic in this modern and mercantile civilization is precisely the object of attack. That "communal" bed, so bold and honest in its emphasis on instinct, also serves to suggest how much we have all lost in our selfish scramble for impersonal deeds, cold cash, private chattels and separate beds.

Otkar had once been logical, willing, honest, and industrious in business affairs; but "like everybody else, he had expected too much of these virtues" (7). In the incredible but happy ending of the story Otkar and the charitable young streetwalker, who have fallen in love, finally escape from the ugly confusion of modern materialism when they discover a belief in life, in kindness, and in generosity. What they actually rediscover, of course, is the familiar Judeo-Christian ethic of simple charity; and what their symbolic escape from New York City in search of a life in the verdant South really suggests is a return to the ancient verities of human experience.

Even if they did not pause to analyze the allegory, thousands of Americans, hungry for some evidence—even for some bare suggestion—that the democratic dream had not turned out to be a nightmare, were delighted by such pity for the unfortunate, by such candid doubts about the sanctity of laissez-faire economics, and by the "naughty" escape in fantasy that the book afforded. A host of readers fondly remember Nathan's gossamer tale and the old serenity it promised long after their first encounter with it during the bleak depression years.

Road of Ages (1935), another topical book, was also written in the special context of the early 1930's when depression abroad prompted disaffected Germans to experiment with a politics of terror. In January, 1933, a coalition of cowed conservatives agreed to make Adolph Hitler the Chancellor of Germany; in February, senile President von Hindenburg served as agent for him in suspending public meetings and in muzzling the German press; a few weeks later the *Reichstag* burned; in March, 1933, legislators, who had been reduced to abject servility, vested Hitler with full dictatorial powers; and promptly thereafter the Nazis began the execution of liberal critics, the suppression of all opposition parties, the destruction of trade unions, and the organized persecution of the Jews.

Nathan does not bother to rehearse this background in his novel, for his basic theme has even older and broader implications. "The Jews were going into exile," he explains, and he uses such ordinary language that the reader almost forgets the ancient terror of his meaning. "Eastward across Europe the great columns moved slowly and with difficulty towards the deserts of Asia, where these unhappy people, driven from all countries of the world, and for the last time in retreat, had been offered a haven by the Mongols" (3). Nathan is dealing, of course, with a recurrent trauma of the human spirit that involves more than any single generation, people, or event. But he attempts no systematic explanation of the social syndrome. Jean-Paul Sartre did that in *Reflections sur la Question Juive* (1946), about a decade later, by defining the anti-Semite as well as the authentic and the inauthentic Jew, ridiculing the prelogical taboo placed upon a people carelessly charged with the killing of a god, challenging the mean complaint that then arose because some of those accused managed to survive by traffic in money, and by denouncing the Manichean fallacy upon which all racial prejudice is based. But Nathan's fiction took ironic notice of most of these issues.

The characters in *Road of Ages* suggest people of every age level, every occupation and profession, every country on the globe—every human being, indeed, who must struggle against an ancient and terrible injustice they have not made themselves and can never fully understand. They are Jews, of course, trapped in the special circumstances of their particular age and perennial heritage; but even martyrdom cannot change their fundamental human nature. "For the Jews had not been made over by their misfortunes; it was impossible for them, even at this time, to agree with one another. Beaten by students, robbed by the peasants, and assaulted by the police of every country, they nevertheless, in the midst of their distress, kept alive their differences of opinion" (5).

So the rabbis of orthodox conviction quarrel with those who hold liberal views except, perhaps, during some tentative truce when they join forces to fend off the atheists; and the Jewish leftists quarrel with the Jewish bankers over questions of profit and ownership that might arise in that wasteland which some of them may never live to see. There is, in short, no single Jewishness in all of these shopkeepers, scholars, farmers, musicians, soldiers, workmen, and their families; but there is indeed a common humanity expressed in their aspirations, suffering, sympathy, and confusion.

This larger irony—man's conscious frustration in trying to govern his terrestrial destiny—best illustrates the timeless implications of the story; for *Road of Ages* makes us wonder again if human vanity has not always been the real source of suffering. In Nathan's modern and quasi-journalistic fantasy, at any rate, we often seem to hear the echoes of an ancient Hebrew scepticism that is much older than its standard definition in Ecclesiastes—that quite unsentimental prophecy which also recognizes the tears of such as are oppressed but have no comforter, and which warns men against the arrogance of their own pride. Opposed to this persistent scepticism we also seem to feel, despite man's new inhumanity to man, an equally ancient joy in life such as the Psalms evoke.

That Nathan meant to resurrect these familiar perspectives is obvious. For his epigraph to the novel Nathan uses Jeremiah's stern reassurance, given so many centuries ago, that the Lord will certainly return the errant seed of Jacob from the lands of their captivity. Indeed, the frequency of biblical allusion, paraphrase, and quotation; the calculated parallels of past and present circumstances; and the sadly prophetic tone—all give the characters and events in *Road of Ages* an ancient relevance. No doubt this recognition of primeval forces still at work in contemporary life affords comfort to many readers. Although some psychoanalysts might construe the novel as just another exercise in psychic masochism,[2] arguing that Jews have always been obliged to seek their victory in defeat,[3] and although a philosopher such as Susanne K. Langer might describe it as prelogical fantasy, an early stage in the symbolic transformation of raw experience into terms of rational definition,[4] Nathan's story clearly avoids a rigorously intellectual approach to the old dilemma of the Jews. It relies instead upon the familiar premises of revelation, prophecy, intuition, and common sense; and most general readers surely respond to the author's fresh affirmation of the joys in living, of the hope that survives suffering, and of the purpose that is eternal. How can they help but remember, as they read Nathan, those ancient promises of escape from pain, despair, and confusion that are formulated and preserved in the Bible?

In his next novel, *The Enchanted Voyage* (1936), Nathan ridicules the notion of escape. Mr. Pecket, disillusioned with worldly affairs and dominated at home by his wife, finds release in dreaming that he is a navigator on the unfettered seas. He builds a sailboat in his backyard, an uncaulked vessel which gradually takes shape in a dreary, waterless world; and he spends his free hours on board. Once in the middle of a dream, Pecket's boat actually "sails" off with him along the busy roads, across the bridges, and down the turnpikes away from Manhattan. "How good life is, he thought, if only a man is given leave to live it. Each for himself, and all for God, that's how it ought to be. But that's not how it is" (90-91). And Pecket understands completely his new circumstance: "Escape—that was it; escape from what he'd done, from what he'd been, from all the fears and doubts which made up his little world" (183).

All the same, he comes to realize that escape is not the real answer, and begins to feel guilty about leaving his wife. Like the Shlemihl he seems to be, Pecket inscribes "Greeting from Valparaiso" on a postcard he mails to her from Beaver Dam, Virginia. When she looks at the postmark, however, she knows just where to look for him. In the meantime, Pecket "sails" into misfortune when his vessel accidentally careens completely off the solid roadway and promptly sinks in the only water it ever encounters. Pecket is obliged to renounce his dreamy life of derring-do. Although the author also includes one of his usual parallel tales about young love triumphant, the love affair between Mary and Mr. Williams is actually subordinate to the adventures of Mr. Pecket.

Nathan obviously sees the humor in man's inveterate attempts to escape from obligation, but he also knows the compulsion is real and often urgent. *One More Spring* was certainly important in bringing its author to wide public notice in 1933, and the comfort that it offers did win him countless friends, but no other book of his will probably ever equal *Portrait of Jennie* (1940) in ultimate popularity. The first of these two novels evokes sympathy for human beings seeking to escape the spectre of hunger, and stresses the importance of social love; but the second extends hope to all who seek escape from death, for it suggests that one true lover exists who can make each of us immortal.

Not that the experience of Jennie Appleton and Eben Adams in the story is entirely divorced from social affairs. "It was a time of depression everywhere," according to Eben's own account of the wintery world of 1938-39. "Hatreds clashed and fought in the air above our heads, like the heavenly battle of angels and demons in the dawn of creation" (19). Nevertheless, the story, for the most part, is far more concerned with the mystery of beauty, the great puzzles of time and eternity, the intangible forces which seem to shape all human destiny, and the power of love.

The design of the story may be likened to the concentric circles formed when a stone is dropped in water, save that there are only two. The smaller circle represents events which make up one year in the life of Eben Adams—events which are described in literal fashion and in the customary time sequence, beginning with a winter night late in 1938-39 when he, an unknown painter, is twenty-eight years old, poor, and hungry. But Eben knows that such facts do not adequately define his problem: "There is another kind of suffering for the artist which is worse than anything a winter, or poverty, can do; it is more like a winter of the mind, in which the life of his genius, the living sap of his work, seems frozen and motionless, caught— perhaps forever—in a season of death; and who knows if spring will ever come again to set it free?" (3-4).

Part of Eben's trouble stems from his choice of subjects to paint, for many of his paintings seem devoid of inspiration—his study of the fisheries at North Truro, for example, or of the church in Mashpee, the new bridge in New York, and of Central Park. The proprietor of the art gallery, at any rate, dismisses all of them as routine landscapes—until he notices a rough sketch Eben has made of the child Jennie; he invites Eben to submit additional studies of her. Whether by accident, by fate, or by inscrutable design young Jennie Appleton thus becomes the means by which Eben escapes, if only for a moment, from that winter of the mind which engulfs him and his work.

At first, he senses nothing unusual about the child. Her clothes are somewhat odd, and she has an awkward habit of vanishing; but the literal cast of Eben's mind is not to be changed so easily, and he is not even inclined to examine the mysterious details. Only slowly does the terrible chill begin to lift from his mind and spirit. But Eben's meetings with Jennie, at irregular intervals during the long winter months, gradually rouse his latent sensibilities, and he becomes conscious of the mystery she represents. He then learns to respond to the beauty of earth, the love in people, and to the challenge in living.

All these changes come to a focus in his desire to paint a meaningful portrait of Jennie—a chaste and haunting portrait of the maiden ever sought, forever dreamed of—the dearly unpossessed of man. In his mind the mystery of Jennie seems to acquire religious significance:

> We think of God, we think of the mystery of the universe, but we do not think about it very much, and we do not really believe that it is a mystery, or that we could not understand it if it were explained to us. Perhaps that is because when all is said and done, we do not really believe in God. In our hearts, we are convinced that it is our world, not His.
>
> How stupid of us. Yet we are created stupid—innocent and ignorant; and it is this ignorance alone which makes it possible for us to live on this earth, in comfort, among the mysteries. Since we do not know, and cannot guess, we need not bother our heads too much to understand. It is innocence which wakes us each morning to a new day, a fresh day, another day in a long chain of days; it is ignorance which makes each of our acts appear to be a new one, and the result of an exercise of will. Without such ignorance, we should perish of terror, frozen and immobile; or, like the old saints who learned the true name of God, go up in a blaze of unbearable vision. (123-24)

Whether Eben's speculation results in something cogent, or simply illustrates an easy anti-intellectualism, a compulsive surrender to mysticism, each reader must decide for himself. To a popular audience of orthodox religious views, the argument Eben uses certainly sounds familiar, and may often be persuasive. To such a critic as Kathleen Nott, however, who examines the dogmatic orthodoxy of such modern figures as T. S. Eliot, Graham

Greene, Dorothy Sayers, and C. S. Lewis in her study, *The Emperor's Clothes* (1958), such simplistic argument is unacceptable. The possession of literary sensibility, she says, does not always imply much power of abstract thought or even much interest in philosophy. Against all those who claim that reason is a separate and inferior function, in comparison with faith, she argues that the ability to reason is based on inference, on attachment to human experience, and so can never provide more than a high approximation of certainty. But our capacity for inference—and thus for increase of real knowledge—has not deteriorated or failed of late. "What our age may have to content itself with learning," says Miss Nott, "is that we *know* not so much and may not soon know very much more, even of what it seems biologically imperative to know. On the other hand, to depart from the method which leads us to knowledge will not make us any less ignorant."[5] Eben's meditations, based on his own cycle of experience, are not likely to impress such intellectuals.

The larger circle of events in the concentric design that we discover in *Portrait of Jennie* represents not one but twenty-eight years in the life of Jennie Appleton. Although the cycle is obviously longer and fuller in Jennie's case, her experience has a pace and sequence of its own; but there are several crucial points when Eben and Jennie share common moments. The double

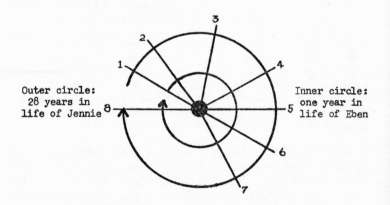

The numbers in this diagram identify distinct episodes which are discussed in text below

time pattern that makes it possible for them to be together at quite different moments in their respective lives is not too difficult to imagine. If a reader thinks of himself as standing on the "bull's-eye" of Nathan's story, looking straight out across the concentric circles of an imagined "target" which then surround him, it is easy to see that Eben—moving round the one-year orbit of the inner circle at conventional speed—consumes the same amount of story time as Jennie. For, though she must move round the twenty-eight-year orbit of the outer circle, all this requires of her is an accelerated speed. As a matter of fact, because both Eben and Jennie do move steadily at their respective speeds around their respective orbits, the reader's line of vision can indeed bisect their separate lives at a common moment which nevertheless has a different temporal meaning for each.

While this description of the time patterns tends to oversimplify the mystery intended, not least by ignoring the sense of infinite experience beyond all mortal reckoning, still it serves to illustrate the order that exists within the novel. Nathan explained some twenty years after publication that he had meant to avoid exact chronology in creating the fantasy world of Jennie Appleton. He particularly left her age, at each of her eight meetings with Eben, a little vague and the year a little inexact. At the time of composition he rather imagined, indeed, that Jennie had first talked with Eben (Episode 1) in the year 1912. This would have made her four years older than she actually proves to be in the story, and nubile in those circumstances where this might be important. But we have recently grown so conscious of the intentional fallacy that our best course of action is to rely on internal evidence. According to the novel, Jennie is lost in a hurricane (Episode 8) on September 22, 1939, at the age of twenty-eight. Perforce born in 1911, she could hardly have been ready to "talk" with Eben (Episode 1) in 1912; and she could scarcely have "known" much about the Kaiser or the European war which did not break out until 1914. It behooves us, therefore, to reconstruct the actual episodes in chronological order.

Episode 1. At their first meeting Eben is already twenty-eight, and for him it is the winter season of 1938-39. Jennie is approximately five, and for her it is probably 1916 (not 1912 as Nathan had somewhat loosely imagined). Her parents are aerialists; she goes to school mornings, being too small to go all day; and, while she admits she cannot tell time very well, she nevertheless seems to realize that "nobody's ready for me" (8). These facts clearly describe a child of kindergarten age. In terms of the fictional design of the novel, Jennie is still very near the beginning of her twenty-eight-year orbit, but she already has the prescience of eternal woman. "I wish," she says to Eben, "you'd wait for me to grow up" (14).

But at the time he is self-engrossed, oppressed by winter and his own creative frustrations, and is quite unready to comprehend a strange child in the park who is living, not in his world of 1938, but in her separate world of 1916. That night as he explains it himself, "I was at the bottom, without money or friends, cold, hungry, and tired, without hope, not knowing where to turn" (6). Is there, indeed, not reason for him to be somewhat startled and aloof, coming upon such a waif, alone at night in the winter park? But he walks a little way with her, and is only mildly puzzled by her guessing what he has in his portfolio, by her reference to a music hall he feels sure was demolished years ago, and by her assumption that the Kaiser is king of Germany.

As a tour de force such a story may be amusing in itself, but Nathan's purpose is quite serious. He seeks to emphasize by means of fantasy the larger unity which encompasses all human experience. Jennie and Eben are apparently on separate orbits, yet those orbits have points of relevance that suggest some design in all that happens. But at first not even Jennie senses this relevance despite her prescience; and so her little song is sad:

> Where I come from
> Nobody knows;
> And where I'm going
> Everything goes.
> The wind blows,
> The sea flows—
> And nobody knows. (13)

Episode 2. Jennie's habit of appearing quite without warning to share an hour or a day with Eben, only to disappear just as abrupt once again, is something he is slow to recognize as part of her occultism. He is also slow to sense other differences in her way of life, such as the different time schedule for her growth. At their second meeting, which occurs as Eben reckons time, only a few weeks later, Jennie is at least seven years old, for she is now aware of those events a youngster might overhear in adult conversation of 1918. She knows, for example, that a war is going on, though she does not know the name of it. "They won't hurt children like me," she asks Eben, "will they?" (51). But she promptly forgets adult problems when she has an opportunity to skate on the frozen lake, drink hot chocolate, and talk about best friends. She exults when Eben promises to include her in the mural he is painting at a restaurant.

Still, Eben does think she is taller than he remembered. "I'm hurrying," she explains (46). Such a cryptic comment does not startle him so much by this time; he thinks Jennie might very well be playing at Cinderella or Snow White. But he does not challenge her for saying that her best friend, Cecily, has died since the last time she saw Eben. "Two years ago," she says quite matter-of-factly (52). As for Eben, he seems almost eager to gloss over any discrepancies that might tend to separate them. "Perhaps there was something strange about it," he admits, "but just the same, it felt altogether right, as though we belonged just there, where we were, together. Our eyes met in a glance of understanding; we looked at each other and smiled, as though we had both had the same thought" (51-52). Even if Jennie were eleven, as Nathan later thought he meant her to be, her behavior is a bit precocious; and, if she really had been only seven, then Eben is quite justified in thinking there is something strange about her.

And yet Eben is less nympholept than skeptic. It is all very well for the curator of the art gallery to say that he sees something of the past in that first sketch of Jennie that he bought from Eben; and perhaps the new sketches Eben brings back from his second encounter with Jennie do remind him, as he says, of something he cannot place—a feeling of being young. The curator talks about the "timeless" quality of woman, but Eben prefers to verify the fact that the Appletons did in fact perform on the tight wire in 1914 and that both husband and wife were killed when the wire broke in 1922.

Episode 3. At their third meeting Jennie is at least nine or ten, presumably entering a Juliet-age of dawning charm. The differences between her and Eben are rapidly disappearing; their chronological worlds are not so far apart; and their interest in one another is much greater. More important still, each seems to understand the growing importance of the other to his own security. Eben asks her to pose for a portrait because, quite obviously, he finds her fascinating; but he also knows that she inspires him to do good work. And Jennie—the all but disembodied spirit who is swept back periodically into some darker void of existence—seizes upon him in the hope of preserving her place and identity. If, even for an instant, he also displays some insecurity, some weakness, she becomes terrified. Her reaction is immediate, for example, when Eben starts to tell her about his own circumstances on the night they first met:

> "I was scared that night I met you. I felt as though I were lost. . . ."
> She cowered down in her chair, and put her hands up as though I were about to strike her. "No," she cried out, "Oh no—don't ever say that, not ever again. And besides, you weren't lost—you were here, and here isn't lost. It can't be; it mustn't be. I couldn't bear it."
> And turning to me almost piteously, she added, "We can't both of us be lost." (84)

For Eben their relationship is at the moment obviously less compulsive. He thinks of her as something more than child, and yet he cannot quite imagine that she is turning into a woman while he watches. Although he now accepts many of the strange things that occur in her presence, he still hangs back from the great enigma she always suggests. After promising to sit for the portrait, she again vanishes.

Episode 4. At their fourth meeting Jennie must be eleven or twelve, for she is still shivering with the terror of what has just happened at Hammerstein's Music Hall in 1922. "It's father and mother," she manages to tell Eben. "They had an accident" (102). One effect of this incident is to sever Jennie's last ties with childhood. "You're all I have now, Eben" (106). In spite of shock and sorrow she sits for him as he begins work on the portrait which is to establish his reputation. The picture needs no description,[6] Eben feels, "for most of you have seen it in the Metropolitan Museum, in New York. It is the picture of a girl somewhere in her early teens, seated in front of a golden screen. The Museum calls it *Girl in a Black Dress*, but to me it has always been simply Jennie" (104).

By this time Eben is about ready to grapple with the mystery Jennie represents. "One must sometimes believe," he now concedes, "what one cannot understand. That is the method of the scientist as well as the mystic: faced with a universe which must be endless and infinite, he accepts it, although he cannot imagine it. For there is no picture in our minds of infinity; somewhere, at the furthermost limits of thought, we never fail to plot its end. Yet—if there is no end? Or if, at the end, we are only back at the beginning again?" (109).

Episode 5. At their fifth meeting Jennie is well into adolescence—almost within the shadow of vigorous young womanhood, as Eben phrases it—and her behavior is now marked by that exuberance, independence, and innocence which characterize these years of transition. Dressed in the uniform of her boarding school—middy blouse and skirt that comes nearly to her ankles, in the fashion of the early 1920's—Jennie prattles excitedly about her life at school. She is enchanted with the friendships, the comings and goings, the daily incidents of the convent society, where she is able to be, for the first time in her life, part of a little community. As she talks, Eben sets to work upon the portrait which he is anxious to complete. Suddenly she asks, in a queerly breathless voice, if he thinks people can sometimes know what lies ahead. But Eben has been half listening, and half ignoring her. She asks her question once again. Still engrossed with his work, and still unaware of how serious she really is, Eben gives an abrupt response which, even as he speaks, he knows is hurting her. Jennie falls quite silent, and in the waning light Eben takes the opportunity to complete the portrait.

In Eben's world, it is the end of winter weather; and, in a symbolic sense, the portrait proves he has also escaped the winter of the mind. But quite by accident he did rebuff Jennie, and this time she leaves only a cryptic note behind when she vanishes. "I'll be back again some day. But not soon. In the spring, I think" (120).

Episode 6. The portrait is finished in March, 1939; and a month later Eben thinks he sees Jennie in a crowd at an art gallery. She is still dressed as she was when they were last together, but now she weeps as she stands before a painting of the Pamet River just where it cuts through the low hills of Cape Cod to empty into the sea. She is gone, however, by the time he reaches the spot.

Eben realizes that as an artist he has reached the moment of fruition. More than ever he attributes this state to love. Although he recently ridiculed Jennie's dark premonitions, he now begins to be obsessed with mysteries. He speculates, for example, about the unique quality of this love they share:

> What is it which makes a man and a woman know that they, of all other men and women in the world, belong to each other? Is it no more than chance and meeting? no more than being alive together in the world at the same time? Is it only a curve of the throat, a line of the chin, the ways the eyes are set, a way of speaking? Or is it something deeper and stranger, something beyond meeting, something beyond chance and fortune? Are there others, in other times of the world, whom we would have loved, who would have loved us? Is there, perhaps, one soul among all others—among all who have lived, the endless generations, from world's end to world's end—who must love us or die? And whom we must love, in turn—whom we must seek all our lives long—headlong and homesick—until the end? (138-39)

Episode 7. At their next meeting the lovers are no longer separated by awkward temporal barriers. Jennie is at least twenty: and, though her private world may still be identified as 1931, she nevertheless can fully share the spring sunshine of Eben's 1939. The new sense of unity that engulfs them makes them conscious of a world forever beautiful, of a harmony in all experience, and of an immortality they may find together. Jennie is so impressed by the new security which seems almost assured that she changes one line in the lonely little song she chanted once for Eben when they first met:

> Where I come from,
> Nobody knows,
> And where I'm going,
> Everything goes.
> The wind blows,
> The sea flows—
> *And God knows.* (156)

No longer is Eben helpless in his winter of the mind; no longer is Jennie lost upon some blind slope of space. It is time for celebration of their love, or so they feel. After a happy picnic day in the fields, they return to spend the night together in Eben's room. The unravished image of the portrait is quite forgotten now in their mortal union. But Jennie and Eben are routed out of bed by an irate landlady whose vehemence is shaped by conventional standards and whose action proves how "ignorant" she is of the transcendental meaning in their love. Deeply frightened and ashamed, Jennie leaves at once. "Good-bye, Eben," she says, "I'll be back again some day—But not like this. Not ever again like this. Not until we can be together always" (163).

Thus spring comes, and is gone. The dream of idyllic mortal love has been humiliated by the doubt, suspicion, and censure of the mundane world. During the late spring and summer Eben broods, works, and waits. "It was then that I longed for Jennie, at such times as these, when the world's beauty fell most upon my heart. And yet, in a way which I found hard to explain, I was not lonely; for I had a sense—as I have had ever since—of not being alone—a feeling that the world and Jennie and I were one, joined together in a unity for which there was no name, an inexpressible one-ness" (185).

Episode 8. At their final meeting, Jennie has reached the age of twenty-eight, and has therefore caught up with Eben. On September 28, 1939, she and Eben find each other for a helpless moment in a hurricane, and are then wrenched apart by the blind forces operating in both realms of time. The visible pattern is at last complete, for in that tragic, fleeting moment their separate orbits coincide—the vast confusions of time and space, the ambiguity of love and identity, the mystery of present joy and eternal hope, are all fused in mystical experience.

For readers who surrender to the verbal melody and the pervasive mood, and who do not cavil at the arguments or pick away at minor details, the story is a delightful melodrama with the most serious kind of overtones. In terms of story design, however, what are the implications? Will the immortal promise in their love prove any easier to realize than the mortal consummation? In terms of simple earth-bound logic their last rendezvous is little more than a freak accident; it is incredible in terms of fact, ironic but scarcely tragic in terms of theory—however plausible in terms of fantasy. Even in terms of the metaphysics Eben had evolved during his long year of mystical gestation, can such a glancing collision between two independent spirits—who then whirl on, as we must suppose from Eben's survival, in their separate orbits—be wholly convincing or genuinely comforting?

A romantic reader might very well think so, for he could with justice believe the lovers will meet again beyond the pale of ordinary time and place, as both Jennie and Eben imply from time to time is their expectation. The story asks, after all, if good marriages are not fated, and if, therefore, true lovers are not justified in searching for each other across all the eons that make up earthly time in order to consummate a perfect union. For the credulous, all such matters can be blurred into affirmation by romantic reverie.

A pious reader could, with equal justice, discover in the novel a parable of that very mystery which Eben comes to appreciate, and might therefore adopt Eben's faith that carnal love, earthly beauty, and mystery itself are evidence of a divine order. The frequent, and sometimmes vehement, passages of pure anti-intellectualism in Eben's narrative would protect him in this interpretation. For those inclined to piety, *Portrait of Jennie* could serve as a secular testament of faith.

A sceptical reader could—by denying the premises of fantasy, by disregarding the siren mood and music, and by refusing to suspend the customary balance of reason and intuition in human judgment—prove the action fraudulent, the tone sentimental, the argument illogical, the language vague, the chronology imprecise, and the thesis utterly mystical. He could, in short, destroy the gossamer thing Nathan so gently constructs.

Portrait of Jennie has been frequently reprinted in the United States, and so far has been translated into Danish, French, German, Italian, Japanese, Portuguese, and Spanish. It was also made into a rather lavish motion picture, which now seems destined to occupy the late show on television for some years to come; and this circumstance very likely means that the story of Jennie and Eben will continue to be Nathan's most popular work so far as the general public is concerned.

III   *The Mystery of Time*

It is perfectly obvious that time plays a major part in all of Nathan's work, not only by permitting him to deal in long perspectives, as in the urban pastorals and other tales of irony, but also by providing a mystical sort of evidence that faith is still in order, as in *Portrait of Jennie*, where merely rational, literal, and conventional human attitudes lead to nothing but a "winter of the mind."

Although Nathan's fantasies have sometimmes been linked to the ontological works of John William Dunne—the British philosopher who published *An Experiment in Time* (1927), *The Serial Universe* (1934), and *The New Immortality* (1938)—there was apparently no conscious borrowing. Nathan explains that he did not read Dunne's work until some time after his own speculations on time had been formulated in fiction. But he did read *The Time Machine,* the novel by H. G. Wells which we have already recognized as an influence on his work; *Tertium Organum* by the Russian novelist of small-town and peasant life, Gleb Ivanovich Ouspensky; and *Four-Dimensional Vistas* by the American theosophist and architect, Claude Bragdon.

All things involving time fascinate Nathan, and *Portrait of Jennie* is simply his best known fictional experiment in time fantasy. The short novel entitled *But Gently Day* (1943) is a more macabre example of the same interest. Nathan says he has always been rather horrified by the prospect of a human brain living on, however briefly, after the rest of the body has given up its struggle against death. *But Gently Day,* while its overt purpose seems to be a demonstration of how the American dream is vested in the beauty of the land, where it serves to inspire patriotism in each succeeding generation, employs this notion of a surviving mind to provide a time-frame. A modern soldier, killed in the crash of a plane bringing him back home from war, returns in fantasy to his ancestral home as it was three generations earlier in pioneer times. There he discovers that beauty, love, and a hope akin to faith were and are the essence of American experience. After this informative retrogression, his still living imagination enters once again the dying, modern body it has briefly survived, content with the enduring sense of purpose in natural order past and present.

Long After Summer (1948) employs another temporal device. An orphan, Johanna, after surviving a childhood spent in dreary institutions, finally has an opportunity to live with relatives in conventional society. In the first spring of this new way of life, she meets a young man with whom she falls in love. Together they share what Nathan calls a long summer of the heart, but in the autumn the young man drowns in an off-shore boating accident. The shock is so severe that Johanna thereafter refuses to think in ordinary time patterns. Autumn now means death to her, whereas spring means that happy beginning when she first discovered love. She begins to act as if the normal cycle of the seasons were just reversed, permitting her to leave death behind and move toward those moments of her greatest joy. Despite this time fantasy, the novel is quite realistic in other details of style and organization. The girl's hallucinations are finally removed and she is able to participate again in the conventional patterns of life.

One of the more adroit manipulations of time in Nathan's work occurs in *The Wilderness Stone* (1961), a semi-autobiographical novel in which he splits his own personality into distinct fictional characters. One is a poet who lives in Greenwich Village during the heady days of literary ferment in the 1920's. Unfortunately he dies, according to the novel, in the early 1930's. The other is a novelist who once shared those glorious days of song and speak-easies with the poet, and who now survives him in a world he thinks has grown both frightened and frightening —a modern, maddening, mundane kind of world which cannot even comprehend the zest with which Americans in the younger decades of the twentieth century lived, worked, and dreamed.

This novelist of the story finds himself in communion, from time to time, with that poet long since dead. They talk often of the years they shared, less often of the present moment, sometimes of the future. But these moments of communion are vague experiences, and the past is not always distinct from the present. In fact, the aging novelist, sometimes called Uncle Edward now, does not always seem to be sure if he is talking with his old friend Bee, the poet, or with his young nephew, Claude. And the poet, Bee, often prefers to ignore temporal categories in favor of more eternal reality. To suggest this kaleidoscopic situation Nathan sometimes creates a stream of consciousness:

> We were all at the Lafayette, in the side room with the black and white marble floor, with the little tables and the chess players. Ray and Coby and Guy and Bee and I, with coffee in front of us on the table, and some red wine in coffee cups, because it was still prohibition. I could hear Coby singing about old Mingolf . . . Ray's song and Guy's: "Mingolf the mighty . . . Hotter than hearths of the herdsmen in winter, Stamped on the Tundra . . . In old Lithuania."
>
> "The Lafayette is gone, Bee," I said. "And so is the Brevoort.

> And Broad's, and the Elevated that made such sharp shadows, and such a clanking thunder."
>
> "Gone?" said Bee; "why, no—it's here, where I am. Like the dinosaur."
>
> "Did you say something, Uncle Edward?" asked Claude.
>
> "No," I said.
>
> Mingolf the Mighty. I could hear the voices, from far away . . . and the sounds of the soft spring night, the motors, the groan of cable cars, the clop-clop of a horse and carriage, the rumble of the Elevated, the singing . . . (42-43)

In this happy instance of style itself creating meaning, the garbled mystery of time is evident in the concurrent patterns of conversation.

The Wilderness Stone also uses the fantasy motif of the lorn-and-roving spirit lover which had proved so popular in the story of Jennie Appleton and Eben Adams. In this instance, however, it is a young man—Bee, the poet—who is adrift in time searching for his fated soul-mate. A young widow, whom the older novelist knows, is the object of Bee's search; she and her child were apparently members of Bee's family in some previous life experience. While the notion of timeless lovers receives considerable emphasis, especially in the conclusion of the novel, the more engaging aspects of the book consist of the comparison and confusion of two separate eras in the impressionistic comments of the narrator. For him, time is egocentric.

In *The Mallot Diaries* (1965) there is an even greater time differential between the patterns of experience which are examined. The novel describes Neanderthals who have managed to survive into the present day and who live for the most part as they always have, with only minor concessions—to missionaries, to carbonated soda, and to the sudden sweep of helicopter patrols that roam today over the Superstition Mountains. Nathan again seeks to create a stereoptic vision by deliberately mingling two modes of human experience, one modern, one paleolithic. When Professor Osgood, an archeologist, and his friend Professor Mallot cross an invisible threshold into this living past they find remarkably little cause for surprise. They participate in a hunt for mammoths with stone-age men who prepare against the accidents that threaten by taking out insurance; an inter-eonic love affair begins to flourish between a modern man and an ancient girl; and teen-agers stage a coup by which they seize control of everything. Professor Osgood observes with scientific reserve that man has not changed in a hundred thousand years, but Professor Mallot cannot resist adding a moral judgment: "He is still a scoundrel" (188). For these two characters time quite obviously is static, unavailing.

And in this fashion Nathan explores the ambiguities of time in one book after another, sometimes as a central theme, more often still in brief, speculative passages. For the most part, he treats time as an absolute mystery which nevertheless serves to dramatize the lonely and ephemeral condition of man and to suggest some larger meaning which man can only take on faith. Since he insists on the importance of ignorance and the significance of genuine mystery, Nathan makes no attempt to develop a rational metaphysics of time in the manner of James Joyce, Virginia Woolf, Thomas Mann, Franz Kafka, or William Faulkner.[7] Nevertheless, he experiments constantly—with accelerated time in *Portrait of Jennie*, suspended time in *But Gently Day*, reversed time in *Long After Summer*, impressionistic time in *The Wilderness Stone*, and expressionistic time in *The Mallot Diaries*. The mystery he evokes is meant to have the efficacy of prayer.

CHAPTER *4*

Dramatic Work

NATHAN first worked for Hollywood in 1943. After six or seven weeks, his stint completed, he returned to New York; but Metro-Goldwyn-Mayer must have liked his work, for he was offered a regular contract as studio writer in 1944. From Nathan's point of view that contract had attractive provisions; so long as he worked at least seven months for the studio in any calendar year he could do as he pleased in his free time. He usually spent the summers writing in his cottage on Cape Cod. Once or twice he did stay in Hollywood year around, but for the most part he was happy to escape to Truro, where the sea and the dunes and the serenity of private occupation offered peace of mind. He describes these Cape Cod summers in *Journal for Josephine* (1943), a memoir in which he tells how the customary calm was punctuated by military activities of a nation at war.

Certainly he found Hollywood different. Some years later in *The Innocent Eve* (1951) Nathan created a fictional portrait of the motion picture producer that was anything but flattering. Mr. Miles Sutro, as he is named, takes luscious young starlets with him everywhere in public, where they are duly ogled and admired. But women are really an old story to Sutro, spending as much time as he does with the loveliest and most eager young women in the world; and he finds among his camellias as much visual satisfaction, and about the same mental stimulation. Actually Sutro has only one weakness, Nathan explains: "an inability to tell the truth; it was an occupational disease" (46). On one occasion, for example, the producer says he has been reading about Mephistopheles, but in reality he had the story of Faust told to him, with appropriate gestures and expression, by a reader at the studio. "It was the only way he ever read anything" (101). And then, as a matter of fact, Sutro was annoyed to think a man would actually sell his soul just to get a girl. When the picture was made, all such nonsense was changed; the modern Faust became head of an advertising agency and got the girl anyway. Sutro feels his taste is beyond challenge:

"It grossed four million six."

"There was a young woman in it," said Lucifer reminiscently, "who, if I am not mistaken, was suffering from an incipient emotional disorder. She was a child star whose successes had gone to her head. The doctors advised against allowing her to play the part of Marguerite, but the studio overruled them."

Mr. Sutro nodded. "She was worth a lot of money to us," he said. "At the box office."

"Where is she now?" asked Lucifer.

Mr. Sutro replied that the young actress was in a lunatic asylum. "Without her," he declared, "we would not have grossed more than three million two.

"It was worth it." (102-3)

I *Nathan as Film Writer*

Although Nathan is inclined now and again to satirize the film industry and its flamboyant moguls in his later fiction, there was of course a time when he felt much more sanguine about the art, the artisans, and the creative opportunities of Hollywood. Peter Kindred, the almost autobiographical hero of his 1920 novel, frankly revels in the dreamworld of the movies; Henry Pennifer, the professional writer of his 1938 novel, *Winter in April*, is a rueful apologist for such popular arts as radio and motion pictures. And, since Nathan readily admits that he, himself, is usually speaking through the mask of the mature protagonist in his books, these fictional expressions take on the force of personal testimony. From his fiction we may infer that, prior to joining the film colony in 1944, he had no more than the customary reservations about this entertainment industry and no less than the customary enthusiasm of those who choose to write for the mass media.

Two years after becoming a studio writer for Metro-Goldwyn-Mayer, he published an account of his new obligations in an article entitled "A Novelist Looks at Hollywood."[1] The title, by emphasizing that what follows is to be an independent writer's estimate of a collective enterprise, not only suggests Nathan's reluctance to give up his private role completely, but also anticipates a discussion which refuses to surrender book-oriented notions of communication even though it deals with the new languages of the mass media.[2]

Assuming, says Nathan, that the craft of novelist would be of little value in writing motion picture scenarios, he came to Hollywood ready to learn a new skill as dramatist but discovered that a picture is not at all like a play. On the contrary, it is like a novel, but a novel to be seen rather than told. As a matter of fact, learning never to entice the ear too much, at the expense of the eye, was one of the most difficult lessons he had to master. Nathan is convinced, nevertheless, that a writer who uses the camera properly, and makes proper use of all the elements of the picture itself, can create the same effect of style in a film as in the most excellent paragraph of prose.

Nor is style the only correspondence: A picture also resembles a novel, he says, by ranging where it pleases, studying the reactions of single characters, and dealing in description and mood, as it follows by means of the camera "the single, unique vision of the writer" (146). He does grant, however, that the quiet and contemplative flow of the novel has no counterpart on the screen; for, when people come together for entertainment, a common pace and rhythm are necessary to achieve the appropriate mass response. And this pace, this rhythm, is something the screen writer does not control since it depends chiefly on direction and cutting.

From a writer's point of view there are, he concedes, still other disadvantages. The novel is itself a complete work of art, but the script is only one part of the final picture. Producer, director, and supervisor often edit the original script; and, once the picture goes into production, everything is further modified by cameramen, the composer, designers, technicians, and actors. In the end the picture belongs to all of them, but in the beginning —from initial conception to completed script—it belongs to the writer.

Nevertheless, the writer may well find disappointment, even heartbreak, waiting for him in Hollywood, because there are so many things he cannot say and so many things he cannot treat. Nathan does not think this is the fault of the industry but one of a youthful art which must appeal, like the first miracle plays, to the full congregation. The screen play or story is a valid form, he insists; and the work of master screen writers, even though it is never published and seldom noticed by critics, represents "some of the best writing done anywhere in the country" (147).

As usual, Nathan's comments on art tend to be more concerned with the artist as a person working on the fabrication of his private vision than with large abstract principles; his major thesis relies on the authority of his own assertion with a minimum of close analysis; and those parallels and differences that he notices in the writing of a novel and the writing of a scenario are reported without benefit of precise definition. Nathan was, of course, addressing a popular audience in his essay which he originally intended as a preface for a script he meant to publish in book form.[3]

Nathan shares credit for writing the screen versions of *Pagan Love Song* and *The Clock;* and, whether credited or not, he had a large hand in a great many other stories.[4] What often happened, however, was that a script upon which one writer had labored for some time would be reassigned to some other writer who had *carte blanche* to alter as he pleased—or as he was instructed by those superior to him in the studio.

An instance of the awkward workings of collaborative method is recounted in Nathan's fictionized autobiography, *The Wilderness Stone,* where he wryly explains why he should be absolved of responsibility for the script of *Pagan Love Song:* "I wrote the script for a motion picture to include Mme Lehmann and the young dancer Cyd Charisse. Mme Lehman was to sing, against the fragrant Tahitian night, the melodies of Schubert and Brahms. After I left the studio, the producer had the script rewritten; it ended up as a water-ballet for Esther Williams, and Mr. Howard Keel did the singing; there was no part for Mme Lehmann" (63).

The case was different in *The Clock,* a film made from a story by Paul Gallico, for Nathan's work on the script helped to make it an important commercial picture. As it happens, James Agee used *The Clock* to illustrate the dangers of relying too much on music in a film, especially when music is used to bind together a block of images which are actually deficient in visual or kinetic relation, which thus permits lazy creation and encourages a Pavlovian response. "The rough equivalent might be," says Agee, "a poet who could dare to read aloud from his work only if the lights were dimmed and some Debussy was on, very low."[5]

As co-author of the script for *The Clock* Nathan was only one of several contributors to the film, all of whom were subject to the direction of Vincent Minelli, yet it seems relevant to point out that several of Nathan's early works of fantasy depend on extrinsic moods which are generated by lyric exposition and which serve as a bridge from chapter to chapter or as a coda for some action so fraught with meaning that mere logic will not express it. Even in such a late and conventionally realistic novel as *A Star in the Wind* (1962), verbal music often serves to summarize a crisis, enlarge the implications of a small event, or knit story fragments into a larger aural tapestry.

Moreover, Nathan's language, first and last, is characterized by a subjunctive mood appropriate to fantasy; he habitually uses such words as *perhaps, almost, as if,* plus all the other conventional devices by which we suggest conditions contrary to fact. His favorite punctuation, indeed, is an ellipsis which he sometimes employs within a context that is not really interrupted, or adds to the end of exposition that is meant to suggest more than it says, or uses to close conversations that need to be infinitely projected in the hope of discovering all that is unspoken and unspeakable, or offers as a reminder to us all of those intangible extensions of reality which Nathan senses on every hand.

Would it not be strange if such a writer as Nathan had not been among the first to sense the fantasy possibilities in Gallico's story? It is true that we cannot prove Nathan's influence on the director, but we are entitled to think it existed; for under Minelli's guidance *The Clock* became a dreamlike fantasy of time, of young love, and of the lurking terrors in an enormous city at time of war, and he laced all these elements of fantasy together with a musical score that felt no reluctance in being sentimental.

For anyone interested in Nathan's technical competence in script-writing there is, among the various papers on deposit at the Beinecke Manuscript Library at Yale, a complete version of his *Bridgit,* an unpublished scenario once scheduled for simultaneous release as a book and as a film in the manner Arthur Miller more recently demonstrated with *The Misfits.* Why a film is not carried to completion may prove vain to ask since so many personalities and problems are involved, but the book did not appear because the film did not.

In 1953 Nathan did publish *The Sleeping Beauty,* a play which presents characters in action with a minimum of exposition. They shift from circumstance to circumstance in just the manner we have been trained to understand in films, and the meaning depends heavily upon ironic contrast, sudden associations or disjunctions, and an illogical reality. Because the visual and aural dimensions are missing, however, it is doubtful if the average reader will understand the power and pace implicit in this work; even the camera cues have been absorbed or obliterated in the process of producing a play for the stage.

If we simply read them, both the unpublished *Bridgit* and the published *The Sleeping Beauty* have in fact the same flat quality we also find in Miller's *The Misfits,* for all these works in their book form avoid the final pace and definition which a director must give his play or his motion picture. There is enough evidence in *The Sleeping Beauty* to indicate, nevertheless, that Nathan understood far more about the esthetics and techniques of film-making than he took the time to set forth in his brief article for the general reader.

II *Film Dramatization of Nathan's Work*

For eight years Nathan was under contract as a screen writer, and thus actively participated in that modern polygenesis of our mass media in which the individual is all but lost in the creative process and where his particular contribution is shaped and reshaped by others. Perhaps it is poetic justice that Nathan's own work eventually became grist for the dream factories and suffered the same reworking by anonymous hands.

The first film to be made from one of his books was *One More Spring,* starring Warner Baxter and Janet Gaynor. When it was released in 1935, Nathan's personal reaction was not enthusiastic; years later he had occasion to say why. "Most of my books," he explained in an interview, "have been failures on film, because the people who made the motion pictures were afraid to present my stories as they were written. *One More Spring* was not a success, as a picture, because they were afraid to make Elizabeth a prostitute. Instead, they made her a dance hall girl, or some such thing." Even after twenty-five years his voice had an edge of annoyance: "They took, really, most of the point out of it. They made a sort of unconvincing comedy. I was not happy— nobody was happy, really. They have never shown it again."[4]

From the perspective of these post-modern days it seems curious to recall that Hollywood was once so prim. For Nathan's presentation of Elizabeth as a girl with a heart so free that she often waived her fee, and as a girl who readily shared one bed with not one but three destitute gentlemen, may actually be the most discreet portrait of a bawd that could have been found in that year when *Tobacco Road* shone in prurient splendor on Broadway; yet when Nathan tried—like Walt Whitman and like Jesus—to show that the lowest human being still deserves respect and love it was Hollywood that sought to escape the challenge. It is an instance that shows the hard integrity in Nathan which is often overlooked because he deals in fantasy.

If Hollywood did too little with *One More Spring,* it did too much with *Portrait of Jennie.* The film starred Jennifer Jones and Joseph Cotten, with Ethel Barrymore in a supporting role. "It should have been a small and lovely story," Nathan recently explained, "but instead Selznick made a great big thing out of it. And he was so afraid people would not understand my use of time that he changed it completely—changed it to a *revenant!*"[6] Such an emphasis, Nathan still believes, on the notion of returning, is a serious distortion of the story.

Not only is his theme warped by simplification of the time fantasy, but Nathan feels the technical values are diminished by a bungled literalism. "They had a perfectly ridiculous storm—with Eben rushing up the the lighthouse, mooing like a calf."[6] In a real hurricane, Nathan insists, the roar of elemental forces becomes so great that you cannot hear another person even if he shouts directly in your ear. "And then this—this sailboat," he continues, "with not so much as a belly in her sail, that comes floating in through all that gale and sea-smother to pile upon the rocks—perfect nonsense!"[6]

The only film made from his books that Nathan really likes is *The Bishop's Wife,* which starred Cary Grant, Loretta Young, and David Niven; Samuel Goldwyn made it in 1947. "Yes, it was a lovely picture," Nathan says reflectively, "but unfortunately Goldwyn did not make any money on it. He was so busy getting medals for *The Best Years of Our Lives,* that for six weeks he did not look at his rushes. When he finally did, he was horrified, because Charles Vidor—the director—had made a farce out of it. Goldwyn stopped production completely, but kept Cary Grant on at full salary. Weeks went by; Teresa Wright bowed out, and Loretta Young took her place."[6] Goldwyn finally called Nathan in to work on the project, but not as a screen writer; he was asked to locate Robert Sherwood and get him to rewrite the script he had done for Vidor. Sherwood reluctantly agreed, but when his revised script was submitted to Goldwyn that gentleman turned it over to Nathan for still more revision. Finally Bobby Koster took over the direction. "He shot the whole thing off the cuff, with a writer sitting behind him on the set to provide dialogue on demand. Well, it came out beautifully—I was delighted with it."[6]

Nathan had quite another reaction to the treatment given *The Enchanted Voyage*. "That was tragic, sickening. Even Zanuck was embarrassed, and when he gets embarrassed it must be something pretty bad."[6] As it happens, most film reviewers also found very little to praise in the motion picture version of Nathan's novel.

Of course many authors have been disappointed by the way their work has been treated by the film industry, and perhaps Nathan's experience was only typical. Still we might have guessed that his fiction could survive the commercial ordeal better than most, for it deals with ideas, images, characters, conflicts, and emotions of the most familiar sort, and is expressed in language and action intended for a general public. Does his work not denounce obvious ills, sympathize with common suffering, and endorse conventional values—all without demanding of his audience a reaction too intense for comfort? Does it not, in the manner of Scripture, propose love as a panacea, and even stress the sublimity of mortal love? Does it not offer the ultimate escape of happy endings, even from situations which have usually defied simple solution? Such fiction must certainly have seemed appropriate raw material for Hollywood in the days of formula entertainment.

But this summary adds up to less than half the truth about Nathan's fiction. There is actually a radical difference between his typical novel and the usual formula screenplay; there is a deep honesty in his sadly beautiful world of fantasy that is not often found in Hollywood entertainments. Nathan's books, despite their ingenuous surfaces, frequent sentimentality, and mystical imprecision, have an ironic awareness and ethical concern; behind his simple stories a reader soon discovers profound sympathy, genuine joy in love and life, and a sense of transcendental awe at the mystery of our existence. Moreover, even in his brightest comedies Nathan introduces some shadow of human pain and confusion, and shadows of this sort Hollywood has not always cared to treat.

III   *Nathan as Playwright*

Motion picture scenarios are not the only form of dramatic writing Nathan has attempted, and Hollywood is not the only place he has been involved in problems of collaboration. *Music at Evening,* an unpublished play he wrote in 1935, was produced in White Plains, New York, in 1937; although the trial run was more than adequate, backers were not ready to gamble with it on Broadway. There were several other unpublished plays, such as *A Family Piece,* that did not even have the benefit of trial performance. In the case of the unpublished *Mephisto and the Mrs,* Shirley Booth was tempted but did not at last undertake to play the lead on Broadway; but Nathan salvaged the central theme and situation for use in a subsequent novel, *The Devil* WITH *Love* (1963), which benefits from the concise characterization, deft dialogue, and dramatic tension carried over from the original play.

Nathan also tried his fortune with musicals, which is not surprising since he enjoys music so much. He does not claim much competence in that field, however, as a letter he sent to John Fall in 1939 demonstrates:

> In my early twenties, just after college, I wrote a good deal of music—about a dozen songs, one or two violin pieces, and a piece in three movements which I grandly called a violin sonata. The songs—some of them—weren't bad; simple, and tuneful, of the "Lieder" type. I used words by Housman, Whitman, and other poets—never my own. No music of mine was ever published; Richard Hale sang one or two of the songs at some of his concerts. They aroused no enthusiasm. I finally stopped trying to write music after I started a symphony, and realized that I just wasn't good enough. This decision was a source of gratification to my father, who was—is—musical enough to realize that I was probably simply wasting time.[7]

In 1950 Nathan dramatized Don Burns's *Messr Marco Polo* and, with music by Bobby Dolan and lyrics by Johnny Mercer, the project very nearly went into major production. And he also dramatized his own 1931 novel, *The Orchid,* for which Vernon Duke supplied a musical score. But musicals are uncertain ventures; none that Nathan participated in found sponsors.

One of his plays has a modest production history. *Jezebel's Husband,* a situation comedy which had its stage debut in New England, ran there with some success in 1952, but since Claude Rains declined to continue in the lead it did not move to New York. Nathan subsequently included the play in a volume entitled *Jezebel's Husband and The Sleeping Beauty* (1953). Although it did not receive Broadway production, the play has been presented elsewhere; in 1963, to choose a recent year at random, *Jezebel's Husband* was on the boards of community theatres which were as far apart as Berlin and Seattle.

Perhaps *Jezebel's Husband* has fared better than Nathan's other plays because it depends so heavily on characters and a basic situation previously tested and found popular in *Jonah,* the best of the author's early short novels. Jonah is the protagonist once again, although he is twenty-seven years older and sadly compromised by trafficking in divination for pay; he is not devoid of independence and idealism, but he permits his wife to dominate him and admits that he no longer hears the voice of God. Jonah's wife Jezebel—not to be confused with the infamous queen whose name she adopted because of its notoriety—is "voracious as a piranha"; she is embittered by the loss of youth and beauty and maintains an impoverished respectability by extracting politic omens from her prophet as required by the king of Israel. Jonah's childhood sweetheart Judith, now a widow with five children and a lonely house by the desert, comes in search of the idealist whom she had once spurned. There are eleven characters in the play, but these three define the basic situation of all mankind in their efforts to acquire spiritual grace, mundane power, or mortal love without understanding in the least the cost and complications that might be involved.

Nathan elects to treat this human condition as comic, and the crisis and resolution of his play approach farce. When Assyrians conquer Israel, Jonah is called upon to prostitute his prophetic reputation for the new regime, but he refuses—thus infuriating Jezebel and pleasing Judith. He escapes the usual consequences of defying a conqueror, however, when the Assyrian discovers that Jezebel—not Jonah—is the astute propagandist behind the prophecies of Israel. She is offered and accepts the Assyrian post her husband just declined. As a consequence of his integrity Jonah discovers, meanwhile, that he can hear the voice of God again; being free of Jezebel, he decides to return not only to a dedicated life of genuine prophecy in the desert but also to his first love, Judith, even though he cannot visit her except on weekends and holidays.

Jezebel's Husband obviously does not depend upon some mighty clash of forces or personalities, does not suggest any titanic struggle within the protagonist himself, does not offer intricate arguments or astounding insights, and does not move us to profound pity, fear, or laughter. Instead the play presents typically inept beings floundering bravely or brashly in the familiar toils of human experience; our real pleasure comes from recognizing the small aspirations and follies which are the dimensions of ordinary life.

Nathan's mellow treatment of the human comedy is also apparent in a more recent play, *Juliet in Mantua* (copyright as an unpublished work 1955; 1965; published 1968), where he offers his own version of the star-crossed affairs of Romeo and Juliet. The Friar Laurence of Nathan's play summarizes the familiar sequence of events that culminate in the tomb in Verona; a grisly tale, he calls it, as writ by Will Shakespeare, who got it from Arthur Brooke, who in turn had it from Bandello—or perhaps Boisteau. "Ah well! Here's the honest truth of it; Bandello never knew that the apothecary, mixing his poisons without prescription and against the law, gave Romeo a simple powder made up of alum and bicarbonate. So there he was when Juliet awoke, with no more than a puckered mouth. Not the first man to seek a hero's death, and end up instead alive and married and headed out of town" (4).

Thus Nathan's play begins where Shakespeare's ends, its first scene in Mantua where the lovers have been in exile for almost ten years waiting vainly for one jealous family or the other to forgive and call them home, and all the while a deliberately barren "Julie" gradually thickens with the years and a playboy "Romie" begins to thump a paunch. Called back at last by the Prince of Verona who hopes terminating their martyrdom may end a vogue among the young of tomb-side trysts, Romeo and Juliet find it difficult to adjust to a married state which is unsupported by either family or by a provident husband. Each of them is tempted to renew a childhood love affair, Romeo with Rosaline—wife of Count Paris, and Juliet with Paris—whose previous encounter with Romeo had not proved fatal after all. When Romeo is caught kissing Rosaline a new duel is instigated, but this time the wives act in concert to take the pistols from their husbands, replace them in the list of honor, discharge all weapons into the air, and thus preserve both peace and love. The play closes on a note of new felicity, with families reconciled, and each young wife happily pregnant.

In the Globe Theatre of Renaissance England *Juliet in Mantua* would never pass for Shakespeare, but on the borsch circuit of contemporary America the play would be relished as a deft situation comedy in the best manner of Robert Nathan. The universal quality of its folk themes, the unheroic nature of its characters, and the sadly comic situation in which man forever blunders through the mystery of his existence, all suggest the courage, patience, and wisdom of the Judeo-Christian heritage —happily illuminated by candid Jewish wit.

CHAPTER 5

Now Blue October

N O DOUBT Hollywood left its mark on Nathan. *The Sleep-ing Beauty*, the play Nathan published in 1953, suggests a musky, artificial, mendacious, frankly primitive way of life with-in the motion picture industry in which a young commissary waitress and a much-jaded star indulge once more in the old lapsarian act, cheapening love with their casual and cynical be-havior. If it is symbolic of the world Nathan found in motion pictures, the portrait is damning. He also comments on the film industry from time to time in several of his later books, but seldom with much love and sometimes without much charity.

Perhaps the experience of writing steadily for the screen had only a modest influence on Nathan's basic style and methods of narration. His later work has less exposition and more dialogue, less introspection and more confrontation, less linear develop-ment and more juxtapositions; but Nathan still is not the master of any structural design save allegory, and continues to make himself the all-but-visible protagonist of every story. As a matter of fact, many of his later works treat the by-now-familiar themes in much the same lyric-and-prophetic fashion he had first de-veloped in the 1920's.

Journey of Tapiola (1938), for example, is a mock-heroic tale in which a Yorkshire terrier sets out in search of fame and ad-venture, journeying down East River on a garbage scow, escap-ing thence to Staten Island, returning later up the Hudson on a ferry only to return at last to the security of his Manhattan home. There are indeed some echoes of the Homer's *Odyssey* and of Voltaire's *Candide,* but the allusions are faint and jocular; and there is no genuine effort to exploit the theme or structure such works might suggest. This adventure in miniature is chiefly an excuse for gentle parody: of critics who decry sentimentality, of the once-popular novels running to more than a thousand pages, and of publishers and literary teas. There is also some intense ridicule of modern greed, and an ironic bit which admits how unpopular anyone becomes if he seeks to tell the truth; but the only persistent theme is the power of love. Some of these emphases had been made before; some would be made again. *Journey of Tapiola* touches but does not develop adult interests; it therefore remains a juvenile work.

In *Tapiola's Brave Regiment* (1941), a sequel, Nathan lampoons Americans who cannot see the clear and present danger of World War II, and who prefer to engage in all manner of arguments and delays rather than to face their obligations. In many respects this brief tale is very like its predecessor, not only in repeating themes and tropes from earlier books, but also in the dainty fashion that it develops issues. But there is implicit in this book a far more terrible truth, one made still more ominous by ironic treatment; for just behind the mockery is the genocide, and just behind the small caricatures are the isolationists who have not yet faced the threat of Hitler. If the first of the *Tapiola* books is a spoof of American grossness, the second is a joke based on a terrible aspect of American provinciality.

So Love Returns (1958) has a writer of children's stories as its central character, and he seems to speak, as Nathan's protagonists often do, for the author himself. "A writer finds a style," he explains, "and he stays in it to the end. He may envy writers their styles which allow them to do the bold things and see the strange places, but if his style is to stay at home, there's no use thinking about it" (9). And this novel demonstrates just how relevant such a comment is to Nathan's own literary practice, for here once again is a modern adaptation of folklore in the manner first developed in such books as *Autumn, The Puppet Master,* and *Jonah;* and here is another instance of a daemon coming to the aid of an artist in the manner already exploited in *Portrait of Jennie.*

A sea-witch called Kathleen sometimes seems to be a mystical reincarnation of the author's dead wife Trina, but she also appears to be no more than an emanation from a story he is in the process of writing for she recognizes the circumstances of that story and finally vanishes when the manuscript is destroyed by a fire. Kathleen has a series of encounters with the artist which gradually materialize into a full night of love, shortly after which she finally disappears according to a formula Jennie Appleton also used. "Nobody knows me," says the sea-witch, in just the lonely tone young Jennie once employed; and, when asked where she lives, Kathleen's reply could just as well have come from Jennie too: "You wouldn't know the place" (54-55). There is also a familiar emphasis on love throughout the novel, where it is identified with joy, with truth, with hope, as the most immortal aspect of this mortal experience, surviving distance, time and death itself. As one character in the story explains, nothing is lost as long as somebody remembers it; and, as the author himself concludes his story, beauty is only altered, never lost. This Keatsian mystique, blended with animistic faith, provides the customary affirmation found in most Nathan stories.

I Dark Tales

Still, there is a growing sobriety in some of the prose Nathan produced during and after his affiliation with the motion picture industry. He seems less inclined to gloss over ugly truths. His novels gradually developed a fuller reference to the disappointments of life, and his exposition included a readier admission of spiritual doubt. *Mr. Whittle and the Morning Star* (1947), for example, is in some respects a fragile fantasy, a bittersweet comedy of human situation rather like its predecessors in terms of obvious humor and ambient patience. It employs what are nothing more than stock figures for its cast—minister, banker, educator, student, spouse; they are foils for the one character, Professor Whittle, who has more than surface dimensions.

Nevertheless, the novel does confront the new and terrifying significance of the atomic bomb. "One day the world was full of light and hope says the author,

> and the next both hope and light were gone. Suddenly and quietly, at vast expense, and to save their own lives, men had learned to turn their enemies into radio-active clouds, into poisonous gases and destructive whirlwinds. It was a desperate paradox, for in learning to destroy others they had invited destruction upon themselves.
>
> Only the firm heart should have such knowledge, only the complete and satisfied heart. But men's spirits had remained as before, as full of gravel as a chicken's gizzard. (17)

His own generation simply baffled Mr. Whittle. "There was nothing you could not do," he mutters, "nothing that was too much for you, except to get along with yourselves and with each other. That was the one thing that was out of the question" (21). When he tries to talk with his neighbors about modern nuclear realities, they only evade the dread issues threatening human survival; they prefer to burrow deeper into their respective lairs of prejudice, ignorance, or apathy. What Mr. Whittle urges in the face of impending disaster does seem a bit old-fashioned. "Either you believe in God," he says, "or you do not; but in either case, there is only one thing to do: for all men, everywhere, to work for the good of all—which is extremely unlikely, in any event." At least the little note of disenchantment sounds modern.

Nathan introduces both celestial and mortal warrants for Mr. Whittle's proposition. Thus God, appearing in the novel as a friendly character who is compassionately involved in man's self-destruction, speaks nonetheless with Old Testament rigor about the human condition. He confides to Mr. Whittle that man makes the best protagonist on earth, but categorically denies that man is capable of understanding such ultimate mysteries as divine love, mundane suffering, or—for that matter—human responsibility. Man has indeed mastered earth and air, the author concedes; and he has even conquered disease, hunger, heat, cold, and silence. But what omniscience still detects in the heart of modern man is an ancient, unreconstructed, arrogant, ignorant, and compulsive spirit of self-assertion. As a consequence, such intimations of immorality as man may sometimes claim are less obvious from a celestial point of view.

Even the implications of the protagonist's own conduct are sobering enough. Mr. Whittle and his wife fall into mutual distrust and antagonism because of their own indiscretions, but they restore connubial harmony by forgiving one another. Thus husband and wife, in learning to get along with themselves and with each other, provide an oversimplified but relevant example of human decency in action. For readers who content themselves with the last thing in a story, this happy resolution could no doubt prove gratifying. God Himself, however, points out to Mr. Whittle that he and his wife in their initial indiscretions have freshly violated moral law. So, even though he means to warn his neighbors against error, the protagonist himself is just as prone to err and just as guilty of repeated irresponsibility as his fellows. Was it not Chaucer's Parson who asked, if gold rust, what shall iron do? If Mr. Whittle is among the best, small wonder God remains sceptical of man.

Another dark fantasy of the mid-century years is *The River Journey* (1949), an allegorical novel about that inevitable moment when death claims one partner in a long-established marriage. Although the subject seems grim, the story evokes hope; for it suggests that love can survive death because it lives on in memory. Nevertheless, the book is riddled with questions seldom treated before in Nathan's prose. Is love ever real? Can two separate human beings, each complex beyond imagination, really hope to merge all of their experience and find that unity in love that the wedding ritual promises, or are lovers always lost to one another from the start? Is love so memorable, in fact, that it deserves to survive in memory? Can the survivor, especially if there are no children, retain a sense of old felicity, of passion and peace; or do all lovers soon forget? When death approaches, will not the dying person find a new obsession in thoughts of eternity? Will not the living person be increasingly fascinated by youth and mortal business? And, even supposing love to be real and immortal because of human memory, does this actually mean so much? What if human sense and sensibility are merely an illusion, one more myopic error in man's appraisal of himself and of the infinite mystery which engulfs him?

Presumably these questions, some of which are explicit in the exposition and in the dialogue of characters, but a majority of which are simply implicit in the situation and action, are duly resolved in the melodramatic conclusion. A casual reader might like to think so, but actually there is an undertone of doubt in *The River Journey* that saves it from sentimentality, and that gives it the tension of partial affirmation pitted against partial surrender to ignorance and doubt.

II   *Dark Melody*

Perhaps the candid doubt, more frequent grief, and growing sense of urgency in some of these novels simply reflect the general climate of the war years. *They Went on Together* (1941) is a pathetic novel about two children and their mother driven to headlong flight by military operations of World War II. An episodic tale, the emphasis is upon the terror and innocence of youngsters discovering dead men for the first time, hearing the brittle rumble of artillery that could kill them, finding themselves separated from their mother for a time in the nightmare world of conflict, and surviving less by conscious effort than by luck and instinct. *The Sea-Gull Cry* (1942) is a novel about displaced persons, in this case a girl of nineteen and her brother who is only seven. They live as squatters on a Cape Cod beach until love brings them within the interest of a young American professor. He asks the girl to marry him and helps rescue the boy from a dark compulsion which prompts him to sail in a tiny boat to Europe to fight the enemy who killed his parents. Both stories are topical, and rely excessively on those public moods that pervade a nation in time of war.

Nathan's verse sometimes echoes these public moods. A sonnet he published in September, 1941, is full of the premonitions common at the time:

> Now blue October, smoky in the sun,
> Must end the long, sweet summer of the heart.
> The last brief visit of the birds is done;
> They sing the autumn songs before they part.
> Listen, how lovely—there's the thrush we heard
> When June was small with roses, and the bending
> Blossom of branches covered nest and bird,
> Singing the summer in, summer unending—
> Give me your hand once more before the night;
> See how the meadows darken with the frost,
> How fades the green that was the summer's light.
> Beauty is only altered, never lost,
> And love, before the cold November rain,
> Will make its summer in the heart again.[1]

Ostensibly a nature lyric, it develops gradually as a meditation upon death and upon a rebirth that is half-promised by the relentless cycle of the seasons, and firmly asserted by the author. The verse generates a blue and smoky mood, a sense of night, of frost, of rain and death, that is also very like the parlous feelings of many Americans in that troubled year before Pearl Harbor. As a matter of fact, Nathan wrote quite a bit of popular verse which treated, in forthright emotion and in moralistic terms, the issues facing a nation on the brink of war.

But the dark temper is nothing new in Nathan's verse. Long before Nazi terror and Japanese duplicity produced a grim psychology of war, he was creating songs that echoed with sorrow

and perennial doubt. His first book of verse, which he published
at the age of twenty-eight, bears the rather somber title of *Youth
Grows Old* (1922); and, while there are several cheerful lyrics
in it expressing joy and hope, the volume as a whole is stained
with rue. The tone of individual pieces is fairly represented by
a verse he reprinted from the *Atlantic Monthly* for July, 1920:

> I am no stranger in the house of pain,
> I am familiar with its every part,
> From the low stile, then up the crooked lane
> To the dark doorway, intimate to my heart.
> Here did I sit with grief and eat his bread,
> Here was I welcomed as misfortune's guest,
> And there's no room but where I've laid my head
> On misery's accommodating breast.
> So sorrow, does my knocking rouse you up?
> Open the door, old mother; it is I.
> Bring grief's good goblet out, the sad, sweet cup,
> Fill it with wine of silence, strong and dry:
> For I've a story to amuse your ears,
> Of youth and hope, of middle age, and tears.[2]

It is popular verse, quite obviously, of the sort universally ig-
nored by serious critics. Employing conventional form, but in
perfunctory fashion, so that the octet represents no dramatic,
ideological, or emotional prelude to the sestet, and emphasizing
end-stopped rhyme, a metronic rhythm, abstract personifications,
didactic exposition, an egocentric focus, and extravagant emotional clichés, it is just as obviously the sort of verse that is
universally admired by the general public. Young poets often
favor this posture of overwhelming grief; in Nathan's case, the
mood anticipates one persistent emphasis in all his verse.

It is true, of course, that self-pity was part of the post-war
syndrome shared by most of "the sad young men," and some of
Nathan's fellow editors on the *Harvard Monthly* had indulged in
precious mannerisms clear back in 1914. John Dos Passos, for
example, had not been ashamed to sign his name to a jejune
piece entitled *The Honor of the Klepht?* E. E. Cummings published stanzas redolent with moonlight, pearls, harps, and other
claptrap that are totally unlike the terse conceits he later wrote.

These men of Harvard Yard quite obviously had not yet been
much impressed by the example of Robert Frost or by the Imag-
ist manifesto issued only a couple of years before by Ezra Pound,

Hilda Doolittle, and Richard Aldington; for their work is cheerfully prolix, desperately maudlin, and thoroughly adolescent. It seems that in *Youth Grows Old* Nathan preserves some of this adolescent college spirit, which has been further saddened perhaps by war and chastened by post-war disillusionment.

For the most part these young writers soon outgrew this pattern, but the mood hangs on with Nathan even after the early style has been refined. His next volume of verse, *A Cedar Box* (1928), takes its title from the chill pun that concludes its principal piece:

> So I go forward to queen's three,
> And in to break the bishop's might;
> Then check. The move is swift and sly;
> The master plays it skilfully.
>
> The game is over, then? Not quite.
> The adversary moves, and I
> Avoid . . . I hope the master knows
> How near he came to losing me.
>
> Once more against the wooden foes
> In angles and in oblique ways—
> Though I grow weary of the blows
> Of pawns, and disappointing shocks,
>
> And wonder sometimes what the game
> Is for, and who it is that plays
> So grimly, since the end's the same—
> A closed and quiet cedar box.[3]

The poem shows improvement in technique; the cloying self-pity of 1920 has been sharply reduced; the abstract personifications have been replaced by a specific set of images; the tendency to feature the poet rather than his insight has nearly been suppressed. In an introduction to this volume, Louis Untermeyer points out, however, that a dark mood is still the dominant feature of Nathan's verse. "There is no belligerence," he says, "or blatancy in this volume. There is, on the other hand, a little sadness, a little shrugging whimsicality, and much wisdom. Underneath the simple contours, one cannot fail to detect that grief for an apathetic world, that racial and unrewarding sympathy which the Germans call *Weltschmerz*."

Nathan's next volume of verse, *Selected Poems* (1935), reprints both sweet and melancholy songs from his earlier collections; but it also offers some new pieces, such as "Atque Vale"—as it was called when *Scribner's* published it in August, 1932—which in this book becomes "Sonnet XXII":

> Where I am going there is no despair.
> The daily tide and current of the breath
> Is there withheld ; there is no weeping there,
> No foe like grief, no enemy like death.
> Where I am going there is neither light
> Nor dark nor joy nor mystery nor fear,
> No songbirds singing in the summer night,
> No flowers folding in the dying year.
> Where I am going there is only peace.
> The tired hand is still and never moves,
> The curving fingers never reach the cup.
> All is forgot, the lover and his loves;
> Even from hope the spirit has release,
> And sorrow like a moth is folded up.[4]

The sonnet illustrates the theory of poetry Nathan sets forth in the foreword to his volume. "When I was young," says Nathan, "poems were loved for their beauty. Designed to stir the heart rather than to tease the mind, they were remembered with emotion, and recited like music. This is a narrow view of poetry, dated and fusty; but it is a view which suited me very well. I believed that music was song, and poetry music. I have not altered that opinion."

Writing in *Scholastic* for May 2, 1936, Dorothy Emerson expresses some reservations about such a theory and practice. Robert Nathan's poems do sing, "and with such lovely ease and grace that the reader is for a while hypnotized into believing them better than they are. For instance, it is only after a number of readings that one notices such trite expressions as 'The day goes down, life's dewy morning done'. The reader may improvise musical phrases from his poems, just as someone at the piano can merge melody with melody until the listener can scarcely guess where one song ends and another begins. For example:

> Where I am going there is no despair
> Can still the flying feathers of my breast
> You also under the moon, Oh dark of hair,
> There shall I find you as I go to rest.

"These lines are picked almost at random. It is possible to compose a whole new sonnet by Robert Nathan by simply taking one line each from fourteen different sonnets, and arranging them to rhyme properly."

Although Miss Emerson does make the linear pattern of Nathan's music obvious, she neglects to stress the unifying power of his mood. This pervasive mood—a suggestion of quiet courage, faintly amused sadness, and hereditary melancholy—is precisely what William Rose Benét emphasizes in his review of *Selected Poems;* for he also feels that mood and music are the essence of Nathan's verse. What he should perhaps have gone on to say is that Nathan's principal limitation is the tendency to blur together sense and sound, to reduce language to a melodic incantation, while seldom providing explicit images. He often uses the most general words for their aural association rather than for any precise denotation, and he rarely conveys the feeling that he is observing any immediate object. The music of his verse, moreover, is so consistently in a minor key that it seems at times to be distorted; yet his sense of grief, of loneliness, and of fear are actually part of the larger drama of his work; they comprise an "everlasting nay" which helps to emphasize his "everlasting yea."

In *A Winter Tide* (1940), where he collects the verse he had written during the troubled period when Americans were trying to ignore events in Europe and Asia during the late 1930's, Nathan presents one sonnet that clearly illustrates the metaphysical conflict that he feels is part of human struggle:

> There is a tide that makes upon the shore
> Continual thunder as the waters leap
> Rising and crying from the ocean floor,
> Roaring and rising from the desolate deep.
> This is no summer current, half asleep;
> This is the night in which the world began,
> This is the dark beyond the outer steep,
> This is the icy enemy of man.
> Stand here awhile beyond the flow and foam,
> And do not tremble. Ocean is not free.
> The fisherman who makes the sea his home
> Knows that the tide must turn again to sea;
> And where these waters tumble wide and bare,
> Children will play, and women sun their hair.[5]

In this instance Nathan is more the psalmist of awe than the hymnist of hope. In the octet, the power and indifference of natural forces suggest an ultimate denial; but in the sestet, the regularity of natural processes suggests a steady affirmation. The poem as a whole says, however, even more; it evokes the contradictory tension of our human condition and thereby suggests that trembling for those who are aware of the clashing forces, is almost a way of life.

Of course, this acute consciousness of contradiction—pain matched with peace, terror with hope, a vast indifference with private identity—does not always dominate his books of verse. *Morning in Iowa* (1944), for example, while it does lament much that Nathan feels we have lost, is nevertheless a panegyric:

> American mountains, how they pull the heart
> Into the wilderness, with Indian names,
> And feathered wars, and lost American sky.
> Lost sky, lost earth, and lost American dream.
> That morning dream that drove us from our beds
> To blaze the forest trace to Tennessee,
> Or cross the Indian wars to Oregon.
> That hope of freedom and that love of land,
> That desert thirst and mountain appetite
> To find somewhere beyond the curve of earth,
> Each to his need,
> Each to his own delight,
> A farm, a ranch, a hill of apple trees.
> That was the dream before they challenged it,
> And made us docile wards of government.
> Perhaps it was a nightmare, not a dream;
> Some say it was. You choose the better name.
> But from the wilderness spirit and the breed,
> Such as we are, we came.[6]

Except for this particular passage, a morning mood characterizes the seven hundred and fifty lines of verse narrative in which Nathan exalts the old pastoral vision, with its cooperative spirit of fellowship, and its stress on the simple dignity of each person. Yet the whole narrative was written, Nathan explains, in the shadow created by the death of his dear friend Stephen Vincent Benét and is, quite frankly, daemon-haunted.

"The year after Steve died," Nathan said in an interview,

> I was still very upset. I was working at Metro then, and had my usual summer off, which I meant to spend on Cape Cod. Going

back there on the train I started writing *Morning in Iowa;* I almost finished the whole thing, right on the train. A week, maybe two weeks, after I got back to Truro it was finished. But it was really a poem of Steve's. It was as though *he* had written it, for it was his style, his rhythms, his way of writing. I could not have done it before, and I could not do it again. It was as though—well, it almost sounds ridiculous—as though *he* had been there, writing it.[7]

In this somewhat mystical fashion Nathan is of course acknowledging the influence of another writer on his own work, but it is worth noting that Benét was more inclined to see the beauty and glory of his country in the living moment, and less inclined to brood upon the lost hopes of yesterday.[8]

The next year Nathan brought out *The Darkening Meadows* (1945), the very title of which betrays his drastic shift back to an older mood. It includes most of the occasional pieces he published in various magazines during World War II. There is a vignette involving a girl who watches a troop train depart into the threat of some oblivion; Nathan's grateful tribute to the fallen Captain Colin Kelly, Jr.; and various exhortations to friends, to foes, and to any who might still be apathetic. Also included is his best-known narrative verse, "Dunkirk," which had been separately published in 1941.

"Dunkirk," too, is reminiscent of Benét's style, for it has an easy narrative swing, a patriotic fervor, and an assumption of historical destiny, as its closing lines illustrate:

> The fog rolled over the harbor key.
> Bess held to the stays, and conned him out.
> And all through the dark, while the Sarah's wake
> Hissed behind him, and vanished in foam,
> There at his side sat Francis Drake,
> And held him true, and steered him home.[9]

It is precisely the sort of heart-felt verse that readers of Whittier and Longfellow readily appreciate.

On the whole, however, *The Darkening Meadows* reveals more about the extrinsic temper of those war years, when public issues were often simplified by fear and anger, than it does about the intrinsic quality of Nathan's characteristic work. Even his memorial, "For Stephen Vincent Benét," while it obviously grew out of intense personal grief, has the sound of a public eulogy:

Freedom from fear, you said; and now you stand,
Free of all mortal care and mortal pain,
Forever part of this American land,
Part of its earth, its furrow and its grain.
One with its sun, and with the arrowy rain,
One with the nation's beauty and its youth;
You will be here when Summer comes again,
As love will be, and innocence, and truth.
Ours was a generation set apart
To walk in shadows at the edge of night.
You gave us only what was in your heart,
Honor and kindness, courage and delight.
We can be free of fear because you went
Singing before us to the Sacrament.[10]

This simple, moving, song of commemoration—one that Benét himself would surely have appreciated—suggests that Nathan was driven back upon his ultimate resources in order to cope with the event. Perhaps the death of his friend was, indeed, more than he could readily endure. Even the prose contribution Nathan made to the spring, 1944, issue of the *Mark Twain Quarterly,* is curiously abstract, addressed to general issues, warm and yet not immediately personal. "Steve could write an American classic," Nathan there recalled,

> like "The Devil and Daniel Webster"— but he could write stories like "Doc Melhorne at the Pearly Gates," and "Glamour," and "Too Early Spring"—stories about integrity, about such things as kindness and bewilderment, about youth and love and heartbreak. I am particularly fond of those stories, because in them he caught something about America that's different from any other country. Some quality of youth and hopefulness that is above all American; something about a spring rain in the city, or the feeling of a November evening, that could only be here, in this country. Something in the dreams and sorrows of young people in love, something in the humor, in the simple stubbornness of a country doctor, that doesn't belong anywhere else.

Nathan's allusions are, quite appropriately, to Benét's published work and therefore deal with a public frame of reference; but, while his inferences are graciously drawn, they seldom lend themselves to close logical analysis. The humane temper Nathan finds in Benét's stories is indeed there for everyone to enjoy, and the meaning and manner do deserve praise, but should we call his personal achievement a national trait?

But then, what does logic have to do with Nathan's deep appreciation of Benét? In his essay he touches on what he thinks are far more relevant things:

> Mortal love—in a way, that was the measure of the man. And in a way, it was his measure of America—what he brought to it, and what he asked of it; that it should be a land of mortal love—not of great phrases, though he, too, could make phrases—not of great names, but of small names, too; not a land for big people, only, but for little ones—where the swift child, the country doctor, the Jew, and the sparrow could all be happy—and secure. He would have had it so, if he could; and, perhaps, because of him, and others like him, some day it will be.

Clearly, then, the prose essay is less an explanation that extends our rational comprehension of Benét than a repetition of the emotional tribute Nathan offers in his sonnet, for in both the author seems intent upon the sublimation of a private sorrow while making a public affirmation. This hint of deliberate cheer in the midst of much that could only be serious, if not depressing, is characteristic of *The Darkening Meadows*.

By the time Nathan brought out the collected edition of his verse, *The Green Leaf* (1950), the more violent forms of war hysteria had subsided, and the regenerative promise in the title of his book could be regarded without irony. At both Hiroshima and Nagasaki the earth was indelibly scarred, but in San Francisco a brave new effort at human cooperation was in the making. Of the nineteen new items Nathan added to his old favorites to make what is his fullest and most representative book of verse, only half a dozen or so harked back to the terrible days of recent conflict. He concentrated most of his effort once again upon the broader mysteries of ordinary experience, where he found not only familiar joy but also terror.

The joy he finds is the sort he had always cherished. There is one new love song, for example, a gentle sonnet, serene as anything he had ever written; it gives a bright margin to the dark spectrum of *The Green Leaf*. A few lines suffice to indicate the quiet charm of unpretentious music:

> This is my love, that I must think of you
> In all the slow small hours of the day,
> Thinking how thus she moves, and how this way
> The sweet mouth trembles, as her lashes do
> When she looks upward . . .[11]

A meditation on natural order, or what Nathan might call the mystery of terrestrial beauty, makes the very earth sound as if it were no more than velvet noise:

> This earth which makes a sound
> Of ever blowing breath,
> Rolling in space, the ground
> Of ceaseless bloom and death,
>
> . . . .
>
> Floats in an empty sky,
> And in an endless hush.[12]

Both the love song and this brief pastoral resurrect an old nineteenth-century mood, achieved through simple description that is almost free of symbolic complications.

For the most part, the post-war world seemed grim to Nathan, and this attitude is reflected in the cumulative mood of the book. Of the older pieces of verse he reprinted in *The Green Leaf,* not more than one in five has a calm or cheerful cast. Of the new verse he introduced, all except the two lyrics mentioned in the preceding paragraph are slightly mordant or morbid. It bothered Nathan, for example, to find that by 1950 Americans had grown so callous. Grateful as people said they were for the recent victory, and regretful too that so many young lives were spent to win it, the public had adopted a curious attitude about their war dead. "Nobody thinks about them anymore," Nathan felt obliged to say.[13] It also annoyed him to find the State Department involved in something very like spurious argument and expedient dealing. Nathan does not specify the errors; it is the trend he abhors. Another verse protests the loss of moral principle:

> . . . I remember when the public state
> Served honor first, and after honor, God;
> We fed the bitter fires of debate,
> But what we said was upright as a rod.
> Today we know not what we do or why.[14]

Such irresponsibility in government, as Nathan thought he saw, and such want of plan or purpose, such deviation from the national traditions which he venerated, drove him to write verse of bald adjuration.

> Kindle again the old American dream,
> The triumph and the pain.
> This was an eagle once, whose sparrow sons
> Peck at the crumbs and quarrel in the grass.[15]

It was far more, he felt, than a national sickness. Looking abroad —at the Argentine in particular—his distress was only compounded. New tyranny, old fraud, and fresh enmity among the nations prompted him to further warnings.

> Carthage is gone, and with Cathay.
> Spain is a dream.
> One after one they die.
> They rose to glory, but they had no friends.[16]

Nathan even predicted in one verse that the last queen of England sat on her throne in 1946.[17] Since he was prophesying, he did not need to be concerned about the male incumbent of the moment; it was the throne itself which he believed was threatened by the corruption he saw everywhere.

When Nathan addresses himself thus to great public questions and secular issues his verse tends to lose its old melodic grace, and to take on a prosy, often strident, and awkwardly omniscient tone. Perhaps it came from imitating the prophets of old. Nathan's indictments are usually too broad for responsible specification, and his remedy of universal love will doubtless sound like crank advice to those charged with control of modern government. Such public protestations might well enjoy a warm reception from those inclined to reductive modes of thinking, but neither as poetry nor as social argument are such verses apt to win much sophisticated attention.

Only when Nathan gave up this soap-box style of declamation, and began to brood on the private implications of what he seems to have recognized as a depersonalized, materialistic, amoral and often rapacious society about to commit mass-suicide with its nuclear bombs, did he seem able to write again the old mournful numbers which speak with some convincing intimacy:

> This is the hour of the tolling bell,
> When the exhausted blood no longer burns,
> And the clear beauty that we loved so well
> Returns no more, Oh never returns.
> While in the secret night around us, hark!
> The sound of time retreating in the dark.[18]

His inner despair becomes, indeed, a sort of repetend, chiming through one verse after another; it is far more convincing than his public ire. "Beauty is past and lost and turned to dust," he is apt to say;[19] and even the most hardened realist must feel the poignancy.

The ugly prospects of the future intensified his habit of recalling good things of the past—his hetero-religious heritage, his beloved democratic dream:

> If we must die in bombing and in dust,
> Seeing our cities broken in their pride,
> Then say of us that heaven was our trust,
> Say that we lived in freedom till we died.[20]

For all his natural love of life, however, Nathan managed to face the increasing possibility of death for himself and for others with a show of resolution. He offers this reassurance: "To be alone in the eternal vast / Is to be woven in the very loom / Of quiet."[21] For those who recognize that despair is essential to beatitude, there is nothing inconsistent in his running argument.

Such in any case was the condition of man as Nathan saw it about mid-point in the twentieth century, and it prompted no ecstasy in him. At least one of the verses he wrote then suggests, of course, that life has been forever difficult for man:

> In childhood lonely and importunate,
> In manhood eager, full of anxious wit,
> His life is but a hunger and a wait,
> From the beginning to the end of it.[22]

Yet there is a catastrophic difference once modern man takes fate into his own inept keeping. All that remains to bring about wholesale destruction is the inevitable accident, the predictable human folly:

> All at an end now, the dream, the rust, the corrosion,
> The long fever and chill,
> Though there is still time to capture, to try to recall
> Something that was important—what was it? Taxes?
> Or Nelson at Trafalgar? Or Rome in her might?
> Or the way we cleared our fields with Connecticut axes?
> Or what somebody said in Galilee, on a hill?
> Whatever it was, I think you had better hurry,

Before it ends, completely, once and for all,
And there is no one left to talk to, and worry,
Not even to ask, Did you hear the last explosion?
Did you see the light?[23]

Nathan quite obviously belongs to what W. H. Auden has called
the "Age of Anxiety." The increasing external pressures made
him look inward, caused him to search for some clue in the
spiritual past, for some present faith, by which he could face a
future that seemed empty, violent, and self-destructive. He
sometimes felt impelled once more to pray:

Oh, if there is a God in all this vast
Design of flesh and dust, this maze of will,
Turn for a moment from the hush above;
Give us again the memory of the past,
The light of April over field and hill,
And childhood's morning with its endless love.[24]

Although there are several joyous things included in *The
Green Leaf*, especially the songs composed before the days of
nuclear despair, this volume of verse is the darkest, most anxious,
and most despondent work that Nathan has thus far published.
It marks the nadir of his feelings. The mood was carried over
into the fiction he was writing: *The Innocent Eve* (1951), published one year later, represents a radical departure from his
customary novel because in it he subjects the folly of mankind to
savage ridicule.

This was a time, then, when the private voice and the public
voice were blended; for the dark mood of Nathan's verse spread
finally to his prose, where it tempered the melodrama, sobered
the fantasy, and increased the dramatic conflicts. Several of
Nathan's subsequent novels have a fuller, more complex, and less
assured meaning as a consequence of his more candid approach
to human experience.

CHAPTER *6*

In Sensible Surrender

NATHAN had never been one to deny the many flaws and failures involved in our human experiment, but in his early fiction he is inclined to gloss over many human follies with an extra emphasis on charity, laughter, or hope. His stress then was on the humane tradition, the power of love, and the virtue of patience, which he considered resources by which man could help to shape his own destiny, if only in the most modest fashion. In his later fiction, however, he is far more ambivalent about the possibility of man's acting as his own agent.

Not that Nathan wholly abandoned the cheerful note that runs so steadily through most of his early novels. *The Married Look* (1950) is a fairly sober account of how a marriage can decline when the partners forget their mutual needs and obligations, but the novel does conclude with the familiar affirmation on the power of love. It argues in effect that, even when marriage reaches middle age, its meaning can be young and invigorating. *The Train in the Meadow* (1953) is also a novel about the immortality that comes with love, expressed in this instance by a fantasy in which a boy and girl exchange cosmic destinations. Even though this switch involves a mutual reversal of mortal and immortal expectations, love teaches them new confidence in some ultimate reunion and justifies this interim change of plans that each finds desirable at the moment.

Sir Henry (1955) has for its hero an aging knight, an inept but kindly gentleman not unlike the mock-heroic figure to be found in Lewis Carroll's second Alice book. Even though Nathan's character never clearly understands his chivalric mission until it is far too late, he feels committed to a quest for some good thing, perhaps the grail. But he is an absolute Shlemihl in rusting armor, a beloved bumbler and victor by accident, who happens thus to win not one but two fair damsels. He takes such little care of them, however, that one is seduced by a sorcerer as he stands by, and the second is forcibly used by a beatnik-knight they meet. The novel is full of the same wry humor of his earlier Barly books, and employs the same deft fantasy of horses, dogs, birds, and insects who offer a running commentary on events.

Sir Henry is even better than its predecessors in the type, because it has more dramatic business between the characters, a fuller situation in which all aspects of the action find a clear focus, and dialogue in which parodox is not dulled with preaching. Everywhere within the book one feels an increase of ironic poise. The parody of T. S. Eliot, of *The Waste Land*, and of the Eliotic imitators who followed him make the fifth chapter delightful, if not profound; similar parodies of such other famous figures as Ernest Hemingway are executed with equal grace and justice. Perhaps one of the most gratifying aspects of the book, however, is the author's laughter at himself—assuming that Henry of Brentwood is indeed a mask for Nathan; by making light of his own vanities, he reminds us of the sympathy all human vanity requires. Although it is a parable about love and death, *Sir Henry* is a warm and tolerant human story, well told, with a positive emphasis.

The Rancho of Little Loves (1956), a more modest piece of work, recounts the story of a heavenly intercession in the affairs of a Las Vegas headwaiter, the girl he keeps in his private brothel, and the hotel where he works. The characters are not convincing, the action is contrived, and the resolution is ridiculous; but the novel is obviously meant to be comic, and the happy ending must be taken as one sort of affirmation. *The Married Man* (1962), a volume of light verse, is cheerful, but undistinguished. In it Nathan explores much the same range of domestic problems that enliven accounts of family life in several of his novels.

I *The Poison of His Grace*

Despite the persistence of good cheer in many of his later works, Nathan certainly exhibits a more sober and sobering view of tradition. He no longer conceives of tradition in such man-shaped, idea-patterned, faith-formed, and earth-centered fashion as before. Gone is that simple didacticism found in *Autumn;* much subdued, though never eradicated, is his sentimental yearning for long-lost yesterdays when love and beauty filled the earth with benediction.

When Nathan wrote *A Star in the Wind* (1962), a fictional account of the impact of Zionism on the life of his friend Josef Shaftel, he demonstrated how tradition may indeed become a living force in the present moment, not necessarily in some rational or even humanistic fashion, but as an elemental power creating a beauty and terror of its own, and shaping men and nations into timeless patterns which as often as not defied real explanation.

Zionism has always been both a political and religious tradition, a thing of faith and social action, with very ancient roots and modern fruits. The frequent captivity of the Jews and their unhappy servitude in various foreign lands served to exaggerate in them man's archetypal hunger for a home. Their dispersion under force, in the centuries before and after Christ, led them to incorporate this desire into the very structure of their culture. Thrice daily in their worship even now the observant petition God to rebuild Zion, and in the marriage ceremony, in the mourning ritual, and at the Passover *Seder* the hope for a Jewish state has for centuries been expressed, even by those who never consciously intended to be political activists in the cause of Zionism.

As a political movement, with primary emphasis on purely secular objectives, Zionism is a phenomenon that began in the late nineteenth century. Its political advocates have argued that a Jewish homeland would secure the welfare of Jews in all parts of the world by offering them spiritual inspiration, cultural dignity, and physical haven in time of need. Political advocates of Zionism have insisted that a nation built upon the principles of social justice in the Jewish tradition could be a living model of ethical responsibility for the whole world to consider, and that the moral teaching of the Hebrew prophets would thus gain a new and larger influence.

But the pursuit of political ends did not really get under way until 1897 when Dr. Theodor Herzl, a young Viennese journalist, led the formal organization of the Zionist movement. Prior to his coordination, the multiple interests of the Jews had usually balked important common action. During the last half of the nineteenth century, for example, Czarist tyranny made Jews in Eastern Europe think the creation of some new political state in

Palestine was imperative, and they asked others to join in the
project; but Jews in Western Europe were not very interested
at that time; only as they came to realize that emancipation had
not really brought an end to anti-Semitism did they begin to
brood again about a homeland. Even when a general program
for Zionism was at last defined there were many who could not
endorse it.

As a form of political action the establishment of a national
refuge for oppressed Jews might indeed seem both wise and
necessary to many troubled people, but there were others—
equally involved in the vast social processes—who feared that
the mere existence of such a state might generate new intoler-
ance within countries where Jews were at the moment un-
molested. As a form of religious duty the resurrection of a holy
center for Judaism might indeed seem crucial to those who saw
their ancient forms of faith steadily eroded by the Gentile
environment, but there were others—equally concerned about
matters of the spirit—who preferred to confront or adopt the
growing pluralism of modern life. There has probably never
been a time or place in which Zionism flourished without controversy.

Certainly the recent establishment of modern Israel by fiat of
the United Nations has not settled the fundamental differences
among the Jews. Those who think of Zionism as the "ingathering
of the exiles" have been delighted by the new state's progress.
As often as not these advocates have previously been living in
lands where bigotry still flourishes; their call for mass repatria-
tion has often seemed unwarranted by Jews resident in happier
circumstances.

In more enlightened parts of the world, at any rate, where
Jews have won and exercise political, economic, social, and
religious freedom, this notion of another great migration has
seemed almost bizarre. In the United States, for example, even
Zionist leaders repudiate such a program; so far, very few Jews
have migrated from America to Israel. Anti-Zionists have found
many reasons, indeed, to resist and contradict the pleas of those
who think a modern Israel is the only option.

As in most complex social processes, the great mass of Jews
tend to settle for less polemic positions. Many moderate Jews do
see in modern Israel a haven for those persecuted, and a bastion
for their distinctive culture; but they prefer to support it from

their established homes in other countries rather than to pioneer in that old desert land which is still surrounded by hostile forces.

At any rate, the ancient hunger for home and the perennial concern with identity were factors which Nathan could scarcely help but feel to be a part of his own heritage. That his particular family lines could be traced back to the dignified Sephardic tradition, on the one hand, and to the commercial power of Ashkenazic tradition, on the other, did not prevent Nathan from feeling sympathy for the average experience of all sorts of Jews. A poem he published in December, 1920, which he later called "Diaspora," is filled with the ancient, aching dream they all shared:

> Thou Israel, on a foreign shore,
> So low, so low, that once was great,
> What altars do thy sons adore?
> The golden calf, the scarlet whore,
> Phoenicia's greed, Assyria's hate.[1]

In 1929 he apostrophized the Jewess for the ageless meaning she represents—the regenerative hope: "Thebes and Jerusalem are in your eyes, / The sea, the desert, and the promised land."[2] She is a maiden shaped by sad and wondrous myth, by suffering perseverance; and Nathan acknowledges in the verse he published in 1933 the price the Jews have paid for all she represents as he rehearses the dark implications of being a chosen people:

> These are the chosen; He has named them all.
> None can escape the poison of His grace,
> Or ever ease the everlasting smart.
> It is for them, the honey and the gall,
> To be wakeful, the abiding race,
> And guard the wells of pity of the heart.[3]

When Nazi terror broke out in Germany in 1938, Nathan recognized an ancient pattern being woven once again into our human tapestry:

> Ay, send them out, the dark ones, into the desert,
> If there is desert enough in all the world
> To hold these lonely few, these trembling goats
> Who take for burden all the sins of flesh
> Into the wilderness.[4]

Nathan does speak sometimes as if the Jewish dream were a practical aspiration which men of good will could realize, and yet he understands full well that factional jealousy, economic difference, political competition, and natural human weakness have time after time confounded both the dreamers and their dream, as his allegory in *The Road of Ages* so clearly demonstrated in 1935. If he was sometimes reluctant to commit himself to any specific attitude or to become involved with any program of a partisan nature, this probably reflected his persistent scepticism about any human plan designed to resolve human problems. He was, moreover, at ease with both Jewish and Christian modes of faith, could claim older roots in American soil than most of his fellow citizens, and cherished the democratic principles.

His reaction to a campaign launched by Charles Raddock was, therefore, predictable. Raddock, who published an article on "Judaism and the 'Lost' Intellectuals" in *The Jewish Forum* for July, 1952, denounced what he felt were superficial "God Books" then being offered to the public as explanations of Jewish faith. He posed at the same time a challenge to all serious scholars, teachers, and writers of the Jewish community in America. He was convinced that many American intellectuals were eager to return to Judaism, and that those who had never strayed should help those prodigals find their way home. Citing evidence of massive conversion to Protestantism (G. K. Chesterton, Giovanni Papini, Sigrid Undset, François Mauriac, Sean O'Faolain, Georges Bernanos, Paul Claudel, T. S. Eliot, Graham Greene, Evelyn Waugh, Thomas Morton) and of an equally impressive conversion to Jewish orthodoxy (Hermann Cohen, Franz Rosenzweig, Else Laker-Schuler, Max Brod, Franz Kafka) in which Henri Bergson, Sholem Asch, Franz Werfel, and Simone Weil were the only "fragrant" instances of Jewish genius gone astray, Raddock argued that things were different with American Jewish intellectuals. Despite their professed nostalgia for some spiritual and cultural alliance, they simply did not find their way home to their ancestral faith. "Unfortunately," Alfred Kazin once said, "as the tissue-thin and merely ethical faith of so many liberal Jews shows, pluralism can be an excuse and synonym for no faith at all." In quoting Kazin, Raddock hoped to discredit the distorted tradition purveyed by the "God Books" and to challenge the ethical pluralism of Jewish intellectuals in America. There really was, he insisted, "no Judaism other than Torah Judaism, and no 'Jewishness' for us except the one which is succinctly and fundamentally expressed in the thirteen cardinals of our faith as formulated (for our daily recital) by Maimonides."

Nathan was one of several invited to respond to this challenge raised by Raddock. His comment appeared in *The Jewish Forum* for September, 1952, as part of a symposium; and this article reveals a basic attitude found also in his verse and fiction:

> I am not, as you so kindly suggest, "a Jewish thinker and literateur." I am simply a born Jew.
>
> Therefore I cannot comment on Mr. Raddock's article, as you ask me to. It moves in fields in which I am not at home, in lands whose language I do not speak. That is my fault, not his.
>
> When the anti-Semites send us to the gas chambers, Mr. Raddock and I will both die, equally vexed and equally disappointed, along with Ludwig Lewisohn and my friend Sholem Asch. The formulae of Maimonides will not help us, any more than Sholem's Mary Mother, or Felix Adler's Ethical Culture. Perhaps Israel herself will help us; but Israel is a political fact, not a formula.
>
> And if there are to be no gas-chambers . . . which is hard to imagine . . . then perhaps Jewishness might be left to develop of itself, as it did (not without prophetic thunder) from the Exodus to Saul, and then again under David and Solomon, and again in the two Exiles, and still again in Spain . . . and finally in America. There was a vast difference between Isaiah and Samuel—and between Obadiah and the saints of Safed. Might there not be at least as great a difference between Maimonides and Heine? Or Jeroboam (the first) and Bernard Baruch?

This tone is hardly that of the militant Zionist. Nathan's religious instinct is obviously intense, as all his books attest; and his faith is rooted deeply in the common theism of Judeo-Christian tradition. But he has always been too eclectic in theory for a rigid sectarian and too tolerant in practice for sanctimonious exclusion. And Nathan's patriotism, as previously noticed, is democratic.

But, if Nathan is no Zionist in the customary sense, still he understands the deep compulsions that are so integral to Jewish history, and which seem to provide a deep, sometimes irrational, motive for Jewish conduct. In the opening passage of *A Star in the Wind* Nathan shows the hunger for home and the yearning for respite that drive the displaced wretches of Europe toward Palestine in 1948:

> Morning rose above the hills of Moab, swept across the sea to Cyprus, and lifted the shadows from the ruins of Berlin and Nuremberg. It touched the faces of Jews behind the barbed

wire of the detention camps at Bremen and Wilhelmshaven, on board old, lumbering freighters in the Mediterranean, and outside the stifling tents of Cyprus, where they waited and brooded in bitter patience, barred from Palestine, the promised land.

Nevertheless, time after time these obstinate remnants of Israel, survivors of Belsen, of Auschwitz, and of Buchenwald, slipped through the barbed wire, eluded their guards, and with their few possessions on their backs stole across frontiers, hid in ditches, and made their way to the waiting steamers in Marseilles, in Villeneuve, in Genoa—only to be seized at Haifa by the British and sent back to Cyprus or to Germany again. (3)

Although the novel opens on this darkly compulsive note, Nathan clearly means *A Star in the Wind* to be a fair, straightforward tale of ordinary people struggling to survive a terrible injustice. The book is, of course, about the old injustice shown to Jews; but Nathan has always been aware of the ironic contradictions in their experience. In his previous fiction he usually dealt with the subject in patient fashion, offered candid exposition, but recommended chiefly love and sympathy. In *Peter Kindred*, we may recall, anti-Semitism becomes the occasion for a stolid sort of grief expressed in exposition and mean behavior; the evil is presented, nevertheless, as a thing endemic to the Jewish boy's way of life. Nathan is still more aloof at times in his early fantasies, where such heroic figures as Noah, Moses, and Jonah are presented more often than not in compassionate caricature. In *There Is Another Heaven*, Nathan maintains esthetic distance by recounting with sad amusement the post-mortal career of a Christianized Jew; and in *Road of Ages* he adopts such catholicity of view that all mankind seems to be guilty of some sort of bigotry. So even though he patently understands the Jewish condition, Nathan typically remains objective when discussing it; he turns the complex issues over with painful candor, yet not without wry humor, a great deal of patience, and still more sympathy.

A Star in the Wind is not always so Olympian. The story of an "uncommitted" Jew who finds meaning in life only when he joins his fellows in building modern Israel is told chiefly from the point of view of its protagonist, Josef Victor; and, as a consequence, both the exposition and the pattern of events are shaped by his own experience and personality. If the book is neither so ironic as *Jonah*, nor so encyclopedic as *Road of Ages*, yet it does have a sharper dramatic focus, a more literal frame of reference, and more explicit issues than many of his earlier books; and all these qualities serve to generate empathy. This very involvement seems to make the novel, for all its objectivity, one man's apologia.

Political implications, for example, are usually defined by characters who are sympathetic to the Jewish cause; the sequence of events is inevitably that known to the protagonist and thus illustrates only what he happens to see of a complicated social crisis. Arab hatred of the Jews—certainly a predictable reaction to any Zionist effort to occupy Palestine—takes on diabolic connotations within such a context. "You go through Alexandria," a fellow journalist warns Josef Victor, "and your life isn't worth *lire sixteen*. Any time they can knock off a Jew, particularly one who's going to cover a war, they'd be only too happy to oblige" (100). And the Jewish agent in Paris, when asked about getting help for Josef from the underground, makes any effort to re-enter Arab territory sound like a desperate gambit. " 'You understand the situation?' he questioned. 'It is like the ancient time, with the hosts of the Egyptians and the Syrians arrayed against us. The Mufti is back in Gaza, and Glubb Pasha does exercises in Jordan with his Arab Legion. Soon England will withdraw from her mandate—if she is to be believed; then the Arabs will proclaim a Jilhad, a Holy War, against us' " (107).

By citing more than once in exposition the numerical odds against successful reoccupation of Palestine, where thirty million Arabs oppose six hundred thousand Jews, the author himself appeals for the sympathy usually given the underdog. By showing how one Jewish elder intercedes—at the risk of his own life—to spare an Arab boy who has briefly escaped custody and threatens a Jewish garrison, the author is also able to suggest the dignity and compassion which Josef Victor sees in the Zionist movement.

The British are also examined from this special bias. The Paris agent for the Jewish underground speaks with untempered bitterness about British interference. " 'We do what we can,' he said at last; 'we take them from the filthy camps, from those countries, where they are still hated, where they are treated like animals, and by secret ways we ship them to Eretz. Sometimes we are lucky, sometimes not; sometimes our ships are hunted down by the British Navy, fired upon and rammed, like the *Exodus,* the passengers sent back to Cyprus or to the German prison camps. You will notice, I said prison camps; they are prisons, and not a holiday for displaced persons' " (108).

Another character in the novel, when reporting the defense of a little Jewish fortress in a letter home, summarizes the charges made from time to time by all the desperate Jews: "There is a plane which comes over two or three times a day to drop its visiting cards on us; and, of course, we have no means of replying. Everything here is surplus, left behind by the great powers either on purpose or in secret, under the table. Except for what Avriel was able to buy in Czechoslovakia. American armor, loaned or sold—who knows?—to Britain, and handed over by her to the Arabs, bombards us; we bind up our wounds with bandages made in the U.S.A., for the American Navy" (293-94). This reporting may indeed be jaundiced, but it is appropriate to the fictional circumstances.

Despite this external realism, the story has its real center in Josef Victor's internal crisis—his reluctant and painful recognition that he cannot escape the consequences of his heritage. He has grown up under the warm pressure of a Jewish family's aspirations. Made to practice the violin back home in Cleveland, young Josef was not just urged to do his best but to excel, as though by sheer exertion he could become another Mischa Elman, another Heifetz. But he reacted in a fit of panic, by running away from his professional debut, fleeing from the waiting audience, escaping from all intolerable family demands and from all social obligation to become lost "in his own darkness, in strange ways, in avenues that didn't go anywhere . . ." (62)

Upon growing up he becomes a journalist, changes his name from Josef to Joseph, and develops a nagging sense of guilt for having turned his back upon his family and their way of life. When he meets a gentile girl called Priscilla in Rome, he is happy for the first time he can remember. But the forces of tradition that inform *A Star in the Wind* are ruthless and primordial. So Joseph is embarrassed to think his lover and his mistress can in fact be anyone like Priscilla, a woman of a different culture, to whom his childhood rituals are simple parts of some unknown game. Priscilla is not upset when she discovers he is a Jew; and, when he demands to know if it makes a difference, she says yes, for now she takes him for something more than ordinary man. Joseph cannot accept a simple relationship; he is, in fact, tormented by his amorous success which seems both a victory and a betrayal.

Engulfing Priscilla and Joseph is the inescapable living past; a magnificence of history she feels everywhere in Rome, linking, holding, shaping all experience; but a spectre of fear and guilt he feels only to deny, though it is defined by his very protestations. It is Priscilla who first recognizes that Joseph cannot escape his heritage, his deep compulsions, his present sense of guilt; and, while they are kneeling before the Bambino during a visit to Santa Maria in Aracoeli, she decides to end their relationship. Even as she comes to this unhappy decision, Joseph suffers a private vision in which some enormous figure who seems to stand behind him, dark, inscrutable, unforgiving, causes him a sudden chill of dismay.

Their love affair is thus presented as a collision of two ancient and impersonal forces; its failure almost seems ordained. For Joseph, the experience is part of that larger problem which has already prompted him to repudiate his family and his kind; so is an incident in Rome where he sees another Jew beaten as the *carabinieri* shrug and watch; and so is his visit to the mass grave where a great slab of concrete covers the tomb of three hundred and thirty-five persons, one hundred of whom were Jews, all killed by the Germans in reprisal for blowing up a Nazi truck— an act of which they were completely innocent. These several things bear upon his problem, if only because he thinks they do. His reaction to advances by a random German harlot in Rome, for example, turns even her sleazy courtesy into old hatred for what she calls the *Judenschwein*. Indeed, he comes to see both friends and strangers as threats, as forces intruding upon his privacy, exposing his private guilt, accusing him of treason to his ancestral obligation and to his living comrades struggling to create a modern Israel.

So Joseph Victor, crumpling slowly under pressures which are unseen but overwhelming, takes another name and smuggles himself into Palestine as a refugee, expecting to report the struggle for Zion. As a reporter he means to keep aloof, to be objective, but then he meets Anna—Anna, the dispossessed and helpless victim of social chaos, the young Jewish widow shielding a small daughter through the nightmare years. And in her company he realizes for the first time what it is like to be homeless— really homeless. Only gradually does he come to recognize her symbolic meaning in his life, but one day it is clear. "If I forget thee, Jerusalem," he says to himself, using the ancient song to define the new relationship he feels with Anna, for it seems to blend past into the present once again, and to make their struggle for life, love, and dignity part of some historical imperative.

But the tradition that gives meaning to his life does not bring pure joy to Joseph Victor. First Anna's little child and then Anna herself are destroyed by war, by the old malignancy of blind violence and hatred that always seem to be a part of Jewish experience. As Joseph watches comrades lower Anna's body into the ground he feels, as never before, the painful irony of the burial ritual and of the ruthless mystery in the tradition it represents: *"Yisga dal v'yiskadesh sh'meh rab bo . . ."* This prayer of responsible surrender concludes her martyrdom and his doubt: "That His name may be exalted."

To suffer is, of course, to change. After the loss of Anna and her child, Joseph's rebel spirit is subdued at last. Wholly committed to the vast and ancient processes of his special heritage, he is ready to join the stiff-necked, hunted, embittered, grieving, but gloriously persisting company who have learned to endure the poison of His grace.

Although *A Star in the Wind* is ostensibly an account of real adventures that befell one Josef Shaftel, as Nathan carefully insists in a prefatory note, and even though the book describes that place and time in which the birth of modern Israel did occur, the implications of the novel go quite beyond the biography of a single person and the chronicle of one historical event. The story is a fictional demonstration of the power vested in tradition. Joseph Victor's final comprehension, in its more modest fashion, is similar to the acceptance Job gained long ago, and what others in years to come must struggle to win again. The author makes acceptance sound simple but essential: "There was nothing mystical about it; he had to learn to accept things as they were, as Menasha accepted them, as Anna had accepted them in the end. *Ewig, ewig* [Always, always] . . . So it had always been and so it would always be. There were no small accidents; all that happened to him had made him what he was, and what he would be . . ." (302-3).

Perhaps we should also notice, in conclusion, that the imaginative form of this full-length novel is a major reason for its sober impact. Unlike some of Nathan's more light-hearted tales of fantasy, *A Star in the Wind* involves a continual confrontation of serious issues which are explicitly identified. The author's penchant for occasional satire, which sometimes seems directed at fairly random targets, is here subordinated to a more deliberate irony that runs steadily through the whole story. His customary apostrophes in lyric prose are also fewer, and they are more functional in terms of the cumulative emotional meaning, since they are more closely integrated with the action and only incidentally express the personal moods of an omniscient author.

Above all Nathan's tricks of plot, made possible in other books by a reliance upon arbitrary manipulation, are excluded from this book. The action seems to be shaped by ancient needs and habits that any serious reader can readily appreciate, even if he has not had a comparable experience himself. And because the meaning is so clearly expressed in the simple, Job-like drama, even readers who share Nathan's own preference for fantasy may well agree that *A Star in the Wind* represents his most substantial literary achievement.

II *To Lie in Darkness and to Rot*

Just as Nathan's evocation of tradition in his later fiction suggests a darkening mystery of forces beyond rational definition, so too his familiar emphasis on love acquires a new sobriety in many of the novels written after 1945. It is true, of course, that nearly all his comments about love have an aura of the macabre, for he conceives of love and death as contradictory elements in the paradox of mortality.

In October, 1935, he published a sonnet—then called "Autumn"—in which he contrasts the regenerative cycle of nature, where fruition promises a future, with the mortal culmination of man himself, whose end can seem so final. The closing lines are enough to identify both theme and mood:

> Now is the time to count the harvest in,
> The grains and fruits, the flowers and the weeds,
> Store all, and make them tidy in the bin
> For use in winter, or for summer seeds.
> But many summer hopes, by man forgot,
> Fall now, to lie in darkness and to rot.[5]

This meditation on the bitter season of the year, as Nathan describes it, when death and the prospect of regeneration are so clearly juxtaposed, is neither sanguine nor pessimistic. If human hopes should end as compost, will they not nourish another season of life? Yet death is always the preamble to such a cycle of growth.

In *The Color of Evening* (1960) Nathan again treats the prospect of death. For the aging protagonist of this short novel, death is frankly terrifying. Max Loeb, as he is called, is far more Hebraistic about the inescapable finality of death than most of Nathan's earlier protagonists had been; the immediate end threatens to obliterate all future possibilities. He has duly considered most of the conventional formulations by which men have tried to explain love and death, but Max Loeb remains sceptical of any explanation based on human speculation: "It seemed to him that the stars and their systems, the roofless firmament, the earth itself, the virus, the oyster, and the elephant, were forever beyond mortal grasp, beyond human understanding. How could the finite mind probe the infinite?" (18-19). Asked, then, why he does not revert to faith, Max Loeb can only plead a lack of it—or plead a faith, rather, in excess of faith; for he professes to doubt nothing and to accept everything, so persuasive does he find the mystery of this universe.

Nevertheless, Max Loeb does fear death; and this emphasis upon fear, upon the dark aspect of the paradox of mortality, makes *The Color of Evening* quite different from Nathan's previous novels about love and death. In *The Puppet Master* Papa Jonas does emphasize that death is implicit in the mutual surrender that lovers always make in favor of the next generation, and the suicide of Mr. Aristotle in that novel is the grimmest sort of answer to those who ask if love calls for any sacrifice; but that allegorical tale avoids extended emphasis on death as an integral part of the mortal cycle begun by love. The happy ending, indeed, is defined by love triumphant. And *Portrait of Jennie*— despite Jennie Appleton's terror at being lost in time, Eben Adams' frustration at being trapped in a winter of the mind, and the fatal ending of their final tryst—also suggests that love counts for more than death in the mortal equation. Indeed, love solves all the mundane problems confronting Jennie and Eben, and even seems to promise them immortality. In *The Color of Evening* all the old ingredients are once again stirred together, but the alchemy is different.

Although there is another winsome waif in the story, the real focus is on Max Loeb, an aging man afraid of death, who feels engulfed by a degenerate modernity. Repelled by the noise of popular music, disgusted with nonrepresentational art, offended by the amorality of new generations, irritated by his own loss of status, he invents a golden yesterday when people had been good and kind—at least part of the time: "A man knew where he was then, and where he was going. Hope was his road, and love his destination. Max Loeb had known where he was. Now he was like a traveler going down hill in twilight, without a home. It was so long since he had seen anyone look at him with love" (21-22). The increased emphasis on geriatric psychology leads all the same to the same old paradox of love and death, for what Max Loeb may need is the rejuvenation enjoyed by those who fall in love. But, a man in his sixties, he is therefore not so apt, though still unmarried, to have many amorous opportunities.

When Halys Smith, a fragile girl of twenty—quondam baby-sitter, waitress, carhop, apple-picker, product demonstrator on local television—falls exhausted from hunger next to Max Loeb's beach fire on the sands of Playa del Rey, the right opportunity seems to materialize; for she is homeless, helpless, and eager for security. After he takes her home to share his modest studio, he thinks of her for some days as a daughter or granddaughter whose company helps to keep night frights away; but then he is startled by an emotion quite unexpected, powerful, and pure.

"But it was also, at the same time, tender and innocent, and like the emotion with which Gounod's Faust first regarded Marguerite; *'Oh, merveille!'* he exclaimed, not realizing what was being offered. Or what there was to pay. How could he?—this same Faust—even if he had been able to remember from so long ago what it was like to be young? The raptures, the ardors, made gentle now, tempered by rheumatism and regret?" (79). The new relationship makes Max Loeb self-conscious, and he reflects on the folly of an old painter in his sixties falling in love with such a youngster as Halys; but he also remembers Rembrandt and Saskia, Modigliani and Jeanne, Renoir and Alice Charigat.

Despite faith of a sort, including a belief in God, Max Loeb had for some time been troubled by the riddles of existence; Halys gives him fresh confidence. His former trust in people also revives, for her ingenuous charm acts as a catalyst to convert suspicion to something milder, cautious hope perhaps, though his new attitude is no Whitmanesque embrace of modern life; Halys reminds him that individual human beings can be lovable.

Quite obviously the didactic impulse, pietistic frame of reference, pastoral similes, and mystical allegory in *The Color of Evening* are very like the elements of love stories Nathan wrote before. There is once again the steady implication that love can solve mortal problems and provide the opportunity for immortality. All the same, Max Loeb is not destined to find an easy resolution to his basic fear in the casual illusions of young love. That sort of callow hope might serve people who have not yet lived enough to face the ultimate paradox of life, who still enjoy the prospect of new adventure but have no retrospect of compromise or defeat. Max Loeb is simply not that young; in the strange equation of love and fear which he recognizes in all mortal experience, he can no longer ignore the significance of the dark quantity.

In the story Max Loeb is forced to confront this reality. His arrangement with Halys is abruptly terminated when she leaves to marry a younger man, his own protégé. Even then, however, in the midst of his sudden disappointment, Max Loeb is able to see that it is not age that stands between them—albeit he sometimes pondered what might befall any marriage on the day a wife reached fifty but found her husband ninety; what really stands between them, he feels, is the thought of death. He can see death; Halys cannot.

Nevertheless, the disappointment serves to restore his judgment. He remains convinced that love is the one miracle of all that nobody can deny—for it demonstrates that some power has us in exceeding care, recurs year after year as young people come to love each other without fail, and provides the one memory which man can take with him into the dark. To Halys he explains that he really feels no animus, for he recognizes that one generation must make room for the next. His explanation is, of course, the simple wisdom found in all folk literature, something Halys should have guessed, something Max Loeb should have remembered sooner. What Nathan actually addresses in *The Color of Evening,* then, is the popular illusion of romantic love as an end in itself, an illusion not always limited to adolescents. The story of Halys and Max Loeb denies the claims of merely egocentric love, with its immature compulsion to take for personal gratification, and insists upon the sacrificial nature of mature love, which requires that lovers surrender not only to each other but also to the inexplicable order of life itself.

III   *A Cockroach Millennium*

There is actually nothing so unusual about any of these later tales in which Nathan dramatizes the loneliness, pain, frustration, fear, and sacrifice of human beings who struggle to preserve their heritage and to abide in love. Had he not, in recommending the good life, always pointed out how much that good life really cost? But, though the themes are familiar ones, there is a shift of emphasis in his later work. Nathan still endorses tradition, but a careful reader can scarcely fail to notice that the humanistic spirit, so ebullient in *Jonah*, has given way to a pious fatalism in *A Star in the Wind*, published thirty-five years later. And, though Nathan still believes in love, the empathy he once provoked for yearning lovers in *Portrait of Jennie* is more apt, in subsequent books, to be for aging people committed to some form of quiet immolation, as in *The River Journey* or *The Color of Evening*. The condition of man, as depicted by Nathan in successive novels over the years, is seen to be ever more tentative, helpless, and dependent upon forces that remain inscrutable.

Sometimes the satirical ploys, the ironic stance, the dramatic paradox of his later fiction suggest an almost fatalistic quality. *The Devil* with *Love* (1963) opens with a proposition that is clearly Nathanesque, attributed though it is to Father Deener, who serves as spokesman for the author in asserting what he calls a "generous view" of the universe: "He saw it as something beyond his comprehension, and the more mysterious it appeared, the more unripe and ignorant he knew himself to be" (4). But, despite obvious similarities between the convictions of this fictional character and those we have long since come to recognize as convictions of the author himself, Father Deener is not immune from satire. An advocate of absolute ignorance, he nevertheless feels obliged to mutter against the dogma of original sin. Gently chided for this inconsistency, Father Deener blandly confesses that he too suffers from intellectual pride. The joke is so gentle, the satire so mild, that many readers may fail to notice that it offers, in miniature, an example of common human weakness.

Father Deener even takes upon himself, as the local agent for his church, the troublesome task of exorcising a demon, Samael of Hod, who has been masquerading in the community as a cardiologist while surreptitiously bartering for a human heart. But, unlike those diabolical confrontations involving Faust and Daniel Webster, the contest between Samael and Father Deener seems hopelessly unequal—even though the demon offers to cooperate in the ritual.[6]

> Father Deener took a deep breath. *"Exorcizamus te,"* he cried, *"omnis immunde spiritus, omnis satanica potestas, omnis incursio infernalis adversarii, omnis legio, omnis congregatio et secta diabolica, in nomine et virtute Domini nostri Jesu"*—here he made the Sign of the Cross—*"Christi, eradicare et effugare a Dei Ecclesia ab animabus ad imaginem Dei conditis ac pretioso divini Agni sanguine redemptis"*—
> Again he made the Sign of the Cross. "Dare go no further, audacious serpent," he exclaimed, "to deceive the human race!"
> "It is beautiful, Father," said Samael quietly, "but it is useless. It is too old-fashioned: it belongs to a more innocent time in history, when good and evil were easily separated into black and white. It is not so simple any more."
> Father Deener bowed his head. "I know," he said (177).

There are moments, obviously, when fallible Father Deener and his entire ecclesiastical machinery appear quite ridiculous.

This satire depends on the same sort of paralogic Nathan has exploited before, notably in *Jonah* where not only man but fox and whale presume to think the most complex meanings can readily be symbolized within the terms of their limited experience. In *The Devil* WITH *Love* this sort of parody has more force because it is more intimately related to actual human affairs.

Consider the bitter humor in Nathan's treatment of the impact nuclear destruction might have on the processes of eternity: In a world in which man seems bent upon the extinction of his kind, for instance, what will be the consequences in purely metaphysical terms? Lucifer himself, according to the gossip in his kingdom, thinks the species Homo sapiens will be succeeded by ants or cockroaches—probably the latter. His minions naturally take increased interest therefore in the insect *Weltanschauung;* for, with the possible exception of Lucifer, the demons seem to think they can only exist in the image of whatever denizens of earth imagine, which is usually the image of the denizens them-selves. In fact, the demons seem to remember all the years they went about in skins of reptiles and, before that, exhibited the gills and fins of fish. The boredom of their existence in the age of trilobites is something Beelzebub has no desire to repeat. So the prospect of a cockroach millennium makes them all conscious of the human image they may be forced to surrender.

Does this prospect explain, perhaps, why Lucifer sends Samael to get a human heart instead of the customary human soul? In part it does, although Lucifer's motives are always too old, too complicated, and too ruthless for any simple explanation. The Dark One says his purpose is quite simple; if he can just discover the way to make men love him as, presumably, they love one another and God, then his old problem in recruiting will be sim-plified. And he admits that all the souls previously garnered have no real value in hell, whereas the human heart—that errant, inno-cent, irrational, half-carnal, half-sublime conundrum—is far more fascinating. In a universe of mystery, where the benevolent power does not shrink from making sin and suffering part of His process, why should the malevolent power be obliged to exclude purity and joy from its designs? Such, at least, are the implica-tions of Nathan's story.

During the negotiations between the demonic forces and Father Deener, this very proposition is put to a test of sorts. The old priest is challenged to prove the scope and sincerity of his charity by thinking of the devil himself with love. An awkward issue, for a churchman at least; Father Deener finally finds it prudent to let the challenge pass. His very silence, naturally, has ironic portent.

More explicit in suggesting that good and evil are distinct, and destined to be forever at odds, is the case of Mary Sebastian who happens to fall in love with the man caught in the demon's bargain. When she offers her own heart freely so that he might keep his, the whole diabolical effort is upset; demons, it turns out, do not know what to do with love even when they have the chance to get it.

But the allegory is not explicit; the metaphysical patterns are sometimes human, sometimes super-human; and, on the whole, they evoke a sense of muddle rather than of mysticism. The novel offers no precise answers for any of the vexing questions that it raises; it argues no formal philosophy, appeals to no orthodox theology, and depends on no scientific theory. Even those biblical myths it incorporates are often shown to be self-contradictory. The demons, for example, despite all their talk about taking the shape of trilobites, fish, reptiles, human beings, ants, or cockroaches, are apparently convinced that Lucifer is really an emanation of God, that lesser demons in turn are emanations of Lucifer, and that they all therefore hold patents diabolical to carry on the darker business of fate. For his part, Lucifer takes it for granted that his function complements that of God.

What answers could philosophy, or religion, or science, or myth really offer to the questions Nathan raises? Are demons the invention of man, the agents of heaven, or autoletic forces? Does modern man have no more feeling than insects? Can carnal love achieve what spiritual love dares not attempt? The questions, the contradictions, and the mystery seem formidable. Paradox is heaped on paradox, but to what end?

Nathan's intent in this respect is not only to engage and entertain the reader, but also to force new considerations upon him. Satirists of every age have used paradox in this way—Cervantes, to make chivalry seem preposterous; Swift, to humiliate human fraud and folly; Anatole France, to explode the claims of orthodoxy. But, as we know, the answer to any question or paradox is already defined by the terms in which either is framed.[7] Nathan framed his to demonstrate the need for humility, the virtue of a wise ignorance in man—another familiar theme. In *Jonah,* he exposes Jewish presumption; in *There Is Another Heaven,* he exposes Protestant presumption; and in *The Devil* wɪᴛʜ *Love* he exposes Catholic presumption. Nearly all of Nathan's books exploit the basic paradox of man, whose assurance always exceeds his art in compassing life. But nowhere is he more insistent about the ultimate mystery of existence than in this version of the Faust legend, for which he uses as a prefatory notice a maxim borrowed from Alexander Courage: "The strength of religion lies not in the unquestionable answer, but in the unanswerable question."

If Nathan's early novels seem to suggest that a proper respect for tradition, love, and patience will provide a meaningful pattern for human life, his later novels seem to suggest that the mystery of being is so great that man's only recourse is a sensible surrender to the powers and patterns that defy explanation.

CHAPTER 7

A Strategy for Man Alone

IN SOME FIFTY VOLUMES published during that turbulent
half century following the outbreak of World War I, Robert
Nathan—gnomic poet, satirist upon occasion, and novelist of the
aching loneliness in man—created a haunting definition of the
human predicament. "Here is the world," he says in one of his
verse meditations, "Take it; but don't be fooled. / It's not what
it seems, this day, this hour, but also / All that has been—yesterday, too, and tomorrow— / More than you see."[1] He expects,
however, that human beings will always be fooled by surface
aspects of the moment, confused at first, and then frightened at
last by the mystery of experience. The primary focus of all his
writing is on the endless ambiguities—the illusions of time, the
sadness in beauty, the cruelty of innocence, the sorrow in love,
the comedy of hope, the isolation in society, the separation from
God—which leave man dangling, ignorant, unpossessed. "How
by himself," says Nathan, "is man upon this earth."[2]

The sense of alienation is common in twentieth-century literature, yet the very frequency with which Nathan treats this topic
identifies it as his private burden. He is not obsessed, however, by
fear or anger; he creates no Ahabs. In fact, he typically writes
lyric verse and prose fantasy for a popular audience in the hope
of stimulating laughter, affection, and hope. Embedded in the
fabric of this entertainment, nevertheless, is a bitter knowledge
akin to that in Ecclesiastes and a mystical hope like that in the
Sermon on the Mount. For his best work reflects a deep concern
over our growing modern anomie: Nathan deplores man's loss of
confidence in his own heritage, his loss of sympathy for fellow
creatures, and his loss of courage in the face of burgeoning mystery. And he opposes the loneliness, the fear, and general dis-
belief of recent times, recommending a return to old traditions
as a standard frame of reference, appealing once more for mortal

love and spiritual charity, and urging an ironic stance against the shocks of fate.

But Nathan's is troubled counsel. He always recognized that his conservative views ran counter to the materialism, the Naturalism, and the nihilism of the twentieth century. Worse yet, he often harbors doubt. While he yearns for a stabilizing tradition, he also recognizes the nonsense that can distort the best of creeds and systems. He prays for love, but also understands the deep perversity of man. He practices the role of stoic, but still succumbs to moods of scorn and pity. He searches for some imaginative pattern upon which to model human life, but with passing years becomes even more conscious of a past that is dead and of a future that is empty. Whenever he speaks in a private voice, as he usually does in verse, his inner doubts are apt to be the motive for his prayer:

> Lord of Souls, if any be
> To hear my prayer: from open doubt,
> From unbelief in Thine and Thee,
> I lift my rusty worship out.[3]

I Tradition

The tension between his public affirmation and his private doubt sometimes gives a very human ambivalence to what he recommends. At one time or another Nathan endorses, for example, three different modes of tradition; yet he has some personal reservations about each of them:

Western Heritage. His first calculated use of tradition as a major element of his fiction occurs in the early fantasies, published in the 1920's, where he argues that the humanistic values of our Western heritage still offer the best available pattern for responsible, modern conduct. In *Autumn* (1921), *The Puppet Master* (1923), and *Jonah* (1925), he seeks to identify those central truths and attitudes defined by Hellenic sense and sensibility, Hebraic piety, Roman Stoicism, Christian love, and medieval humility which he thinks still relevant today.

While Nathan certainly has what T. S. Eliot calls "historical sense"—an understanding of the influence of the past upon the present—as a beginning writer he seems to have found this easier to affirm than demonstrate. Even a selective exposition of some major tradition could overwhelm the dramatic illusion of his fiction as, regrettably, it does in *Autumn*. Excessive stress on the parallels of past and present could shrink the complexity of human experience to abstract allegory, as *The Puppet Master* demonstrates. Only *Jonah*, that delightful probe into the tangled adolescence of Ancient Hebrew life and belief, suggests the perennial force that may be vested in tradition.

And even *Jonah*, although it does endorse the traditional Hebraic values, is nevertheless concerned with showing how the best of systems may still fail because, being human inventions, they are always imperfect. As a matter of fact, what Nathan best succeeds in making credible in *Jonah* is not so much the ancient tradition of the Jews as the private frustrations of one particular man.

American Dream. During the 1930's and the 1940's Nathan became engrossed in the more immediate traditions of his own country as its democratic way of life was challenged at home by economic failure and abroad by global war. Of course his early books, such as *Peter Kindred* (1920), *Autumn* (1921), and *The Woodcutter's House* (1927), denounce the gross complication and corruption of the American dream; but not until *One More Spring* (1933) is there a sustained assault on urban, industrial, commercial, and hedonistic forces at work in modern society— forces that Nathan feels have contributed to the demoralization and bankruptcy of the time. In *The Innocent Eve* (1951) the selfish materialism of modern American policy is shown to be reflected in the motives and methods of all the nations who have dealings with the newest leader of the West.

But reservations about contemporary trends did not keep Nathan from raising the alarm when America was threatened from abroad. In verse, in brief satirical pieces, and at strategic moments in his longer works of fiction, he denounces the genocidal madness of Hitler, pledges support to the free world in its struggle for survival, and pays tribute to those who fell defending the traditions of liberty. His most famous ballad, "Dunkirk" (1941) is about the British withdrawal under Nazi bombardment; with the music and temper of Longfellow's patriotic verse, it speaks for freedom in old-fashioned sincerity that generations of Americans have cherished. The novel *But Gently Day* (1945) is an effort to show, by means of serious fantasy, that a modern soldier's last "great measure of devotion" is never wasted. Each generation, according to this book, must in its turn be both a debtor to the past and a donor to the future; each person serves, however humbly, as a living link in the great chain of American destiny. So even sacrifices that seem pointless within the context of any given moment are actually significant to the cumulative national achievement. The very land which lives again each spring, despite the deadly winter, is symbolic evidence, Nathan says, of the hidden purpose that characterizes the American experience.

Sometimes in verse he sounds less assured. One of Nathan's most charming evocations of the special time, the special place, and the special mood contributing to the American dream is the narrative verse of *Morning in Iowa* (1944). Even that volume, however, in spite of its bright title, old pride, and confident music, is shadowed by the logic of the author's observations. He feels obliged to say that the dream has all but disappeared today; it has been crushed by a monolithic state, and drowned in the impersonal tides of mass society.

The Judeo-Christian Ethos. Nothing is more obvious from first to last in Nathan's writing than his deep concern with the basic values, issues, and visions which have evolved from Jewish and Christian experience over the centuries. To list the major points of mutual interest shared by these two religions is to identify Nathan's recurrent themes. Both Jews and Christians hold the Old Testament in high regard; Nathan employs characters, themes, and situations borrowed from this source as a major feaure of more than half his books. Both stress the fatherhood of one God; he everywhere expounds the same doctrine. Both respect the sanctity of the Ten Commandments; he uses them as the moral framework for all his work. Both admire the wisdom of the prophets; he dramatizes them, quotes them, and interprets them in at least a dozen books. Both seek to foster the brotherhood of man; he never wrote a book in which this is not part of his deliberate intent. Both emphasize the spirit of man; he takes every occasion to insist upon the ultimate importance of the spirit.

The sectarian differences that divide these two religious groups frequently provide the ironic humor of his fiction. A Jewish tendency to take pride in being a chosen people and a Christian tendency to condone persecution, while each may be cause for bitter comment in *A Star in the Wind* (1962), are more often treated as the curious proof of man's comic limitations. As a matter of fact, Nathan is even more apt to see the humor in the common failings of all parties, as in our compulsive urge to indulge in iconography of ourselves. But whether sectarian or universal, the flaws Nathan sees in human nature are usually those which have also been identified in the Bible, and often with less humor and charity.

Archetypal Patterns. During the 1950's and the 1960's Nathan's writing began to reflect a growing occupation with still another kind of tradition. Much less rational than anything in the Western heritage, far more ancient than the American dream, and sometimes more Jewish than Christian in its definition of mundane experience, this tradition finds expression in the archetypal patterns of his work. Of course, any reference to archetypal patterns makes us think first of Carl G. Jung, the Swiss psychologist who postulated the existence of a collective unconscious in the minds of men. It was, he said, psychic residua from the past, which is often identifiable in dreams, myths, and literature. Presumably, this common resource permits an author and his readers to share in a common reaction to certain age-old patterns, or "archetypes" as Jung called them, which have been developed by the countless, typical experiences of our ancestors, as in being born, escaping danger, finding love, and facing death. Although many people cannot accept Jung's explanation of psychic inheritance, scholars have identified many recurrent patterns in literature which seem to correspond to the archetypes described by him.

Nathan often touches on the irrational patterns in human behavior, but he seldom undertakes to explain them in psychological terms. His image of woman, seen first in one aspect and then another, runs like some primordial paradigm through all his work. His early novels, for example, often present woman in the image of eternal temptress—fair agent of dark unreason—whose penchant is to lure men into folly, failure, and frustration. Thus, in *Peter Kindred* (1920), a campus wife leads her creative husband off to the banal drudgery of writing advertising copy; in *The Puppet Master* (1923), a vivacious flirt drives her spouse to suicide; in *Jonah* (1925), a sweet conformist helps the young prophet to apostasy; and in *The Woodcutter's House* (1927), a pristine innocent proves so distracting that her swain destroys the druidical trees he worships.

The novels written during the 1930's, however, are more inclined to present woman in another image—as the great fructifying spirit, capable of teaching man to appreciate his human lot and of quickening his sensibility. In *One More Spring* (1933), a girl restores man's confidence in the possibilities of ordinary life; in *Portrait of Jennie* (1940), a girl releases man's imagination from a winter of the mind.

Nathan's still more recent novels emphasize a third, and still more mystical, image of woman. Her mortal love has always seemed to provide man with his best clue to the motives behind all cosmic process, if only by analogy; and so this mortal love also suggests a transition to some more ideal and satisfying devotion. In *Mr. Whittle and the Morning Star* (1947), mortal love is described as the last best hope of modern, secular, and alienated man who waits so apathetically for nuclear extinction in a world where God has been forgotten. In *A Star in the Wind* (1962), mortal love provides the catalyst by which one man feels he can fuse his life into the ancient rhythms of timeless experience.

The image of woman seems to become more complex in Nathan's later fiction, but he was always aware of the contradictions that are so much a part of her archetypal pattern. A good deal of the sad humor in his fiction grows out of the chagrin man always feels in confronting such mysteries as the innocent *femme fatale* whose primeval force he both praises and scorns, envies and fears. And Nathan's image of God, of the devil, and of man are equally ambiguous, suggesting the cumulative definitions provided by human experience through the ages, but acknowledging the complexity such archetypal patterns nevertheless entail. With this ambiguity in mind, we are better able to appreciate his use of such typically Hebraic types as the secular rabbi, the pious sceptic, and the lovable Shlemihl. Nathan recognizes in such contradictory patterns the oldest, saddest, funniest, and most universal truths about man. To recognize the human predicament for what it is, he insists in one book after another, is the beginning of wisdom; for this recognition leads to acceptance and sympathy for others.

II *Love*

Valuable as it must be for Western man to understand his heritage, practical as it must be for Americans to share in the aspirations of their nation, comforting as it must be for modern man to have an ethical tradition deriving from Bible times, and amusing as it must be for rational man to think that his behavior is largely shaped by primeval impulses, these are not really topics of major concern to Nathan. His primary purpose in writing, as far as it may be inferred from close reading of his work, seems to be to foster deeper sympathy between man and woman, between man and mankind, between man and nature, and ultimately between man and God. Both in prose and verse Nathan steadily insists that love is the motive, the means, and the end of being.

Love of Man and Woman. The mortal love of man and woman, a major theme in more than thirty of his books, provides the subject for frequent remark in all the rest. One of the things Nathan does best is to conjure up the miracle, the enraptured moments, and the wild surmise when love startles two more human beings into ecstacy. Part of this success is due to the simple formula he nearly always uses.

In his love stories, for example, the ingénues are often very young girls, innocent, ethereal, with a child's clean hunger for emotional experience. His Amy May of 1923, his Metabel of 1927, his Ellen of 1938, and his Sylvia of 1941 are children; and his Judith of 1925, his Jennie of 1940, his Penelope of 1947, his Halys of 1960, and his Penrhyd of 1964 have barely reached nubility. Nathan's fascination with these green maidens is always circumspect, however, even when he depicts some Elizabeth or Conchita who is not always circumspect herself. And this focus on girls at the moment of their emotional awakening reflects Nathan's characteristic view of love as a wonderful but saddening experience.

When a young woman finally emerges from her Edenic stage of development, as Nathan thinks she does upon discovering mortal love, she is suddenly embroiled in adult frustrations. Her own ingenuous expectations being so deeply passionate, for example, she is much confused by the dispassionate pose which men cultivate. She soon discovers, too, what men consider practicality; but the average woman, says Nathan, while she wants security, is enchanted by romance; and she therefore marries an actor or poet, expecting to be embraced by a Satyr. She is inevitably disappointed, and so is he; whereupon each sets out to make the other over. But, even though they still dream of shaping their separate identities into a single union, neither can really change; and so they remain singular, isolated, and lonely even in marriage. In such works as *The Enchanted Voyage* (1936) and *Jezebel's Husband* (1953) Nathan introduces this theme in a comic perspective; in *The River Journey* (1949) and *The Married Look* (1950), he develops the same theme from a sadly ironic point of view.

Love is, indeed, an incipient form of death, as Nathan frequently points out—a ruthless, sacrificial mystery in which lovers give up their youth, even their very lives, in order to propagate another generation that they will only briefly know and perhaps never comprehend. Nevertheless, love offers immense joy and consolation. In *The Color of Evening* (1960), the author causes Max Loeb to explain how love functions as a miracle.

> "Why," he said, "the way young people come to love each other, year after year, here or in history, wherever they are. We're so accustomed to it that we never give it a thought. But isn't it the one miracle of all that nobody can deny? to tell us what we have to know, that some power has us in exceeding care?"
> "Is it love you mean?" she asked.
> "What else?" he asked. "What else can a man take into the dark with him, but the memory of it, old or young?" (210)

Implicit in this passage, and explicit in a hundred similar comments scattered through Nathan's other books, is the notion that mortal love is a match of specific human beings who are fated by God to meet even if this meeting be delayed a while because they happen to live at different times in history, and that their eventual rendezvous will not only bring them incredible earthly joy but also insure the execution of His grand design in which man has a principal role. The union of true lovers offers proof of God's benevolent interest in human affairs, and provides the man and woman with a memory of natural grace so pure and powerful that in this memory they enjoy immortality.

Nathan usually describes mortal love in terms of mystery and miracle, and nowhere provides a detailed account of his metaphysics. Some readers reject his mysticism, some assent in the paralogism it seems to codify, and some recognize a modern and secular definition of Hebraic-Christian belief that man's hope for salvation lies in cooperation with the omnipotent Lord of the universe, in whose godhead men may participate through righteousness and love in the service of his fellow creatures. At any rate, the implication of a larger meaning gives all of Nathan's love stories an aura of mystery, the tension of aching joy, and a hint of profundity. By virtue of faith in mortal love young Jennie Appleton feels she can defy the paradox of time, the dying Minerva Parkinson is able to face her last river journey with composure, and the young starlet Mary Ann dares to match her innocence against all the guile of Satan.

Love of Man for Mankind. When it comes to human society in general and to the love man owes mankind, Nathan is less hopeful. He is convinced that writers have a special role in creating an atmosphere in which such love can flourish. *Winter in April* (1938) contains an interview between a hopeful young writer and the protagonist, an established author whose views must surely be those of Nathan himself. Upon learning that the young man feels compelled to write about simple kindness, the author meditates:

> Kindness: what a strange word to find on anybody's lips these days. It is like a style in clothes which is no longer worn, or a musty language no longer spoken. What can one do with such a word? It is an instrument which has lost its usefulness. It is of no use either to the hero, or to the commune; it is an attribute neither of the lion nor of the ant. At best it is a feeble virtue; and it has no part in history, for history is made by force. Nevertheless, it has a way of returning every now and then to earth, when one least expects it. The military bands stop a moment for breath, the hunters pause to sleep . . . and there is kindness again, nestling stubbornly in people's hearts, lifting a small peaceful voice, ready for the millennium. (198)

Kindness is certainly a principal emphasis in Nathan's own books. He does ridicule some city hucksters, rural bigots, greedy bankers, a clerical quack or two, various shrews, poseurs, literary critics, the heads of Fascist states, Hollywood moguls, Naturalistic writers, modern non-objective painters and non-melodic musicians, the British on Cyprus, the isolationists in America, as well as himself; but he does so without malice. Except for *The Innocent Eve* (1951), Nathan's censure is typically engulfed in a sad but patient love expressed in gentle exposition, allegorical action, and familiar prose rhythms and diction which often achieve the aural peace that we associate, perhaps, with the Psalms.

Love of Man for Nature. The love of man and woman, as well as the love of man for mankind, prepares the way for a love of nature, that still larger bolus of God's creative beneficence. According to one Jewish tradition, in fact, to express love for animals who obviously cannot be expected to repay it is more virtuous than to express love for human beings. Nathan gives this notion lyrical statement in the prose of *Jonah* (1925), where old Naaman is trying to answer bitter questions by the young prophet: "Naaman replied gently and inexorably, 'my son, the love of earth is holy, the love that God bears the least of his creatures, without desire, without envy, and without malice. That mercy and generosity with which the sun warms and the soil nourishes its flowers and trees, is holy; all that gives of itself, without reason, without measure, and without return. For that is the way of God; it is the way of the One, from which all things spring, to which all things return'" (152).

Such a statement may represent no more than the hope of poets and prophets; indeed Nathan himself recognized how fragile such prophetic statements sound once the poetic mood has passed. His foreword to the 1934 English edition of *Jonah* is written from the perspective of another decade, after the author was forty years of age: "No amount of exercise in writing can bring back a poetry which has been lost, a beauty, an enthusiasm of heart which belonged to what seems—at this distance—almost another person. Here, obviously, in Jonah, is the young man I used to be; and here is the way he wrote. I cannot write like that any more."

Very likely Nathan's second thoughts about *Jonah* were tempered by the times. By 1934, Hitler's savagery was infecting all of Germany; and even the early Nazi behavior was enough to shake any sensitive person's confidence in the power of love, the fraternity of man, and a benevolent natural order. Certainly Nathan felt terrible doubts within himself, as his verse in private voice so amply demonstrates; and yet he continued to encourage readers to love nature and nature's God. Father Deener, in *The Devil* with *Love* (1963), is only one of several characters—laymen as well as clerics—who share a common sense of teleology in Nathan's later fiction: "It is true, he thought: eternity is all around us; we are in it, and yet we cannot see it. We cannot see God, either. Yet I can love the silent night and the heavens lit by stars whose size I cannot measure, and whose distance, one from another, is beyond imagining. And so I should love God; and so I do love Him, though all I have ever seen of Him is this this world beneath my feet and the heavens overhead" (181). The emphasis on nature survives, quite obviously, and yet in Nathan's later books nature has a different meaning. Where he once referred to the purposive, harmonious, and benevolent aspects of nature in rather confident fashion, much as to say that man can shape his life by such tangible precedents, he is more apt in later years to be impressed by the absolute mystery of all phenomena.

Love of Man for God. All lesser forms of love Nathan treats as access to divine love. The mortal love of man and woman he shows as culminating in the immortal miracle of infinite new generations; the kindness man exhibits for his fellow man he explains as the origin of a social beatitude that represents piety in action; the sympathy man feels for nature makes him privy to the mysteries of God's works. In this cumulative sense love of earth proves holy, and Nathan always writes with this mystical conviction. The whole body of his work, he once remarked, could be described as variations on a theme: "It's better to love than not to love."

III *Satire*

But the days of man are few and ever full of trouble. While tradition may offer guidance and love may promise peace, man still needs to be ready for adversity. The ambiguity of mortal life calls for patience, and Nathan's is apparent in his ironic stance, in the balance he strikes between ridicule and sympathy. His particular sense of balance has not, of course, always pleased his critics. Some reviewers have called him a master of satirical fantasy, and some of his books deserve the praise; others have accused him of blatant sentimentality. The characteristic tone of his best work is a mixture of mild satire and gentle sympathy, that culminates in mystical wonder.

Indeed, Nathan thinks of himself as an ironist, rather than as a satirist. He is wont to say that he is somewhat handicapped by centuries of the rabbinate in his family background. "I have a great deal of anger," he once said in an interview; "but I don't like to express it, for I would rather offer people consolation. I have great compassion for the human race.—Oh, I have written satires. For instance, *Road of Ages* is a satire, a bitter book; and *The Innocent Eve* is a bitter book; and there are certainly bitter flashes in my other books. But this compassion I feel dwarfs anger, subdues it, and that is what keeps me from being a good satirist."[4] This statement of intent illustrates the distinction between his public statement and his private attitude, but it does not clearly define the range or nuance of his tone.

Ridicule of Unconventional Behavior. Nathan frequently satirizes what he considers egocentric values and abnormal conduct. This sort of satire, according to Northrup Frye, whose comments in *Anatomy of Criticism* provide the frame of reference for the following discussion of Nathan's satire and irony,[5] usually takes for granted that the world is full of queer accidents, fraud, injustice, and futility—usually assumes, in fact, that there is no possibility of changing these hard circumstances. Therefore it implies that men must learn the truth about human nature, must avoid illusion and compulsive action, and must accept conventions without question since they codify the rough lessons of experience. The key figure in this type of satire is apt to be a plain, commonsense, conventional person who manages to discredit his opponents by slyly demonstrating how they fail to meet common standards.

Certainly Nathan's fiction often takes for granted that the human condition is, at bottom, a frustrating mystery. His typical characters are enchanted by the beauty of their universe, and find joy and hope in mortal love; yet they are usually lonely, threatened, and helpless too; they are awed by forces they do not comprehend and starved for some tradition that can provide the social peace and private dignity often missing from their own lives.

And the key figure in several of his books is a homespun conservative on the order of Edward Noyes Westcott's David Harum or of Mark Twain's Connecticut Yankee in King Arthur's court. While Nathan's protagonist is seldom the spokesman for any large consensus within the story, he does represent the conventional Judeo-Christian values which Nathan and many of his readers presumably share. Although the character seldom prevails in public affairs—witness the public impotence of Jeminy in *Autumn,* Jonas in *The Puppet Master,* Lindeman in *The Fiddler in Barly,* Otkar in *One More Spring,* Whittle in *Mr. Whittle and the Morning Star*—the protagonist in each instance wins significant private victories. He either learns himself, or teaches his partners in the story, that it is both good and necessary to accept the beautiful but imperfect world as it is, to offer sympathy, to practice patience, and to look beyond one's self for the nexus of meaning in life.

Although Nathan usually employs a masculine character in this role, his most effective novels within this satirical mode are *The Bishop's Wife, The Innocent Eve,* and *The Devil* WITH *Love,* all of which ridicule some unconventional pattern of belief or conduct by measuring it against the instinctive goodness of an elemental woman. The ready love and ingenuous trust of a feminine spirit can stir envy in angels, despair in demons, and humility in man. So far as Nathan is concerned, the instinctive kindness in woman seems to represent an ultimate standard of human behaviour.

Ridicule of Conventional Behavior. While the proper kind of conventions may be essential to human welfare, there are times when conventional behavior is nevertheless improper. Nathan sometimes feels obliged to challenge the premises of social custom when he thinks they represent no more than fossil habit, and to oppose the notion that standards can be extracted from human experience which is always more complex than any formulation that purports to explain it. This sort of satire usually manages to ridicule stereotypes, dead belief, crank theories, superstitious terror, and dogmatism simply by holding them up against the complicated reality they presume to explain, or by concocting mock-systems that demonstrate how silly conventions prove to be when examined in a fresh perspective.

Nathan's story of young Jonah is a deft mockery of sterile conventions, and many of his later books are based on this satirical ploy. The ridicule of blindly conventional behavior by means of an elaborately developed mock-system is what makes *There Is Another Heaven* (1929) such a happy tour de force. He uses variations of this satirical technique in *The Puppet Master* (1923) to deflate romantic illusions about marriage; *Jonah* (1925), to challenge the presumptions held by or about a chosen people; *The Bishop's Wife* (1928), to make light of human misconception about the angelic nature; *There Is Another Heaven* (1929), to deride the museum concept of religion and the utilitarian dream of heaven; *Tapiola's Brave Regiment* (1941), to unmask American isolationism on the brink of World War II;

The Innocent Eve (1951), to ridicule purblind international efforts at nuclear control; and in *The Fair* (1964), to illustrate how asinine racial segregation always proves to be.

Ridicule of Human Folly. The capacity of man to act against his own interest, whether by flouting the wisdom incorporated in sensible conventions, or by embracing forms which no longer hold any wisdom, was always obvious to Nathan; but his ridicule of this wrongheadedness is seldom savage. Only in bitter flashes —to use his own phrase—does he ever ridicule human dignity.

The satirical approach that challenges common sense, denies that sense data are actually reliable, doubts that customary experience offers adequate ground for interpreting life, and questions the possibility of real human dignity is simply foreign to Nathan's temperament. When shaped by the furious genius of Jonathan Swift, such satire can be devastating; it exposes the flaws of common sense by gross exaggeration, humiliates the human being by denying him the customary screens of privacy, and overwhelms all polite objection by the sheer vigor of blunt indictment. Nathan sometimes toyed with such artillery, but he lacked the killer instinct necessary for a massive assault.

Even *The Innocent Eve* (1951), the allegorical novel in which he has Satan convene a random cross-section of humanity— builder; socialite; journalist; dress-designer; literary critic; movie producer; starlet; lovers; airforce officer; diplomats from England, France, and Russia; and the anti-Semitic Mr. Rankin from Mississippi—in order to gratify their various appetites and thereby gain control of them and their diabolical atomic bomb is forthright in exposing the selfish, frightened, ruthless, and blindly destructive compulsions which seem to drive most men and women; but it concludes nevertheless in an absolute triumph of the human spirit; and this book is probably the most aggressive satire Nathan ever wrote.

IV *Irony*

Far more characteristic of Nathan are those moments in his verse and fiction when ridicule is more than matched by sympathy, when paradox leads the reader beyond amusement to moot reflection.

Irony of the Human Condition. The most obvious sort of sympathy to be found in his fiction relates to characters who are

trapped by life, possessed by love, confronted by death, and en-
thralled by mystery. In the stories in which this ironic emphasis
is developed, the central figure is neither comic nor heroic;
he is a person of rather normal aspirations and talent who is
obliged to struggle most against the limitations of his own human condition. There are often social or psychological reasons
for this person's dilemma, but these reasons frequently prove to
be typical of the average human experience.

Nathan's effective use of the Shlemihl grows out of this ironic
comprehension, for the ultimate importance of Mr. Pecket in
The Enchanted Voyage (1936) or of Henry of Brentwood in *Sir
Henry* (1955) depends upon a reader's recognition of both the
common humanity and the predictable folly such a character
combines. It is hard to think of a single major character in his
fiction who does not betray, sooner or later, the tragi-comical
limitations of his species; As a matter of fact, these "moments
of truth" typically measure out the principal development within
a Nathan story in which recognition of man's curious predicament represents the beginning of wisdom.

All of his novels depend upon this ironic perspective, but none
is more poignant, when it comes to pleading sympathy for the
condition of man, than the fantasy he so appropriately called
Road of Ages (1935): In this work even the bitterest persecution
is sadly understood to be a function of elemental human nature.

Irony of Fate. Hard as it must always seem to man, he is
obliged to struggle thus against his intrinsic limitations; but it
must seem much harder still to contend with the extrinsic forces
of a fate he never comprehends. From time to time Nathan introduces this darker sense of irony into his work, most often in
his brooding verse, but also in the fictional episodes where he
illustrates how the cycle of events, operating without malice or
remorse, can sometimes crush the human beings caught within
its path.

When writing in this ironic temper, Nathan is inclined to urge
a patient acceptance of the inevitable, but not in a spirit of
abject surrender to blind accident, and not as a denial of faith in
some supernal order, but rather in the patient manner of Job.
He never ceases to hope that humanity will persist even if it
cannot prevail. *Road of Ages* describes a cruel inertia that has
warped the hearts of men for countless generations, and other
books describe human beings who are hurt or deeply frightened,

but Nathan simply refuses to acknowledge any stark reality that human love and simple piety cannot endure.

Perhaps the closest he ever comes to fatalistic comment is *The Weans* (1960), a humorous essay in science fiction written ostensibly by Nat Obelgerst-Levy, Archeol. D., who lives some five or six thousand years in the future during the cultural ascendancy of Kenya, Uganda, and other African centers of learning. At one level, this mock-scholarship seems only to ridicule once more the witless fads of Americans by subjecting them to scrutiny in the hypothetical perspective of six millennia. But underlying the genial satire of a culture engrossed in mere amusement is a more serious tone, an ironic hint of fate, for *The Weans* not only lampoons Americans for their apparent addiction to gossip, rock-and-roll, baseball statistics, premature sex, and elaborate plumbing, but also charges them with failure in those endeavors in which they pretend to be most serious. Obelgerst-Levy, at any rate, finds no evidence during his excavations on the barren western continent that its people ever fostered good music, recognizable art, intelligible literature, or higher studies in physics and mathematics. And he feels obliged to think, on the basis of fragmentary domestic judgments he discovers, that marriage among the Weans must have been a loveless and usually predatory adventure.

What gives this slim volume its most curious implications is the ironic context. Even the greatest societies suffer a diminution when examined against the enormous background of all recorded history; and Nathan makes American culture seem more vulnerable than most when, even in jocular fashion, it is treated thus. "So far," says Obelgerst-Levy, "We have been able to do little more than scratch the surface of life in WE or US. There is no answer to the riddle: who were the Weans? and no solution to the mystery of their disappearance. They left no pyramids, like the Egyptians; no laws, like the Romans; no temples, like the Greeks; no God, like the Jews. Their gravestones are simply mounds on the Great West Continent" (48).

Man still proposes, and fate still disposes, not only in *The Weans* (1960), but also in *Peter Kindred* (1920), *Portrait of Jennie* (1940), *But Gently Day* (1943), *The Sleeping Beauty* (1953), *A Star in the Wind* (1962), and in several of Nathan's darker sonnets. When he speaks in a public voice, Nathan is inclined to identify the wheel of fate with some divine purpose;

when he speaks in a private voice, he is more apt to ask than answer, more likely to brood in doubt or hope in wonder.

Irony of Nothingness. Yet *The Weans* is never solemn and rarely bitter or disillusioned; it is dedicated, after all, to a reader with the gift of laughter. The sense of humor we nearly always find in Nathan's fiction suggests his own refusal to succumb to the mystery he sees on every side. He does not indulge in the ultimate forms of satire—the kind that utterly denounces mankind for willful failure; and he does not engage in the ultimate forms of irony—the kind that sees all human hope and effort shattered by the painful, ugly, amoral, and illogical accidents of life, and that conceives of man as a prisoner in some mad existence where suffering never leads to glory but only to some empty and unnoticed death.

Nathan does subject various religious rites and symbols to parody from time to time, but he respects the spiritual essence they were meant to define. There are no demented, depraved, or hopelessly despondent human beings in any of his books. The world he describes in *Road of Ages*, grim and ugly as it is, and the conduct he illustrates in *The Innocent Eve,* mean and vicious as much of it is, never equal the cosmic terror and depraved behavior in George Orwell's *1984.* Such naked irony is alien to Nathan's work. The persistent undertone in all his books, a motif in minor key, is a blend of pity, piety, and patience; for Nathan, like the psalmists of old, broods on the frailty of man; but he is also awed by the evidence of omnipotence, and so practices the ancient art of acceptance on faith. It is the hard price for a rich mortality that he gladly pays:

> This beauty that will never come again,
> This little heaven that we call the earth,
> Is made to bloom by kindness and men's love
> But only once, that I have knowledge of.[6]

V *Fantasy*

The principal technique of Nathan's most characteristic work is fantasy, and his best results come from his skill in imaginative displacement—particularly in the adaptation of biblical myth and metaphor to the cannons of contemporary secular order and popular taste.

Actually the word "fantasy" has both literary and psychological implications, as C. S. Lewis pointed out in *An Experiment in Criticism*. As a literary term, it has been loosely used to describe any narrative that deals with impossibles and preternaturals; as a psychological term, it has commonly been used to describe a variety of pathological and healthy states of mind.[7] Since literary fantasy does not necessarily correspond to psychological fantasy, the distinctions are worth noting.

Fantasy of Delusion. If some patient were to become so engrossed in some psychological fantasy, let us say the private conviction of being endlessly pursued by killers, that he constantly mistakes this imagined persecution for reality, his case might be described as pathological delusion. But any delusion of this intensity, being wholly private in the first place, can contribute nothing to the public art of literature where some meaningful communion is expected. Although Franz Kafka, to name one of many, has employed some such pattern of delusion in his imaginative constructs, he did so consciously to convey a public meaning by means of a metaphorical system. In the case of Nathan, who feels the alienation of man, but is appalled by the very possibility of the nothingness Existential writers often posit, a pathological delusion could offer very little help; his fantasy owes nothing to this psychological pattern.

Fantasy of Illusion. If another sort of patient were to find so much pleasure in the fantasy of a waking dream in which he never suffers disappointment that he constantly indulges in it to the detriment of his health, even though he does not confuse his obsessive dreaming with reality, his case might be described as pathological illusion. This psychological experience is also a private affair that has very little to do with literary experience. Even those stories which seem to derive a substantial part of their formal meaning from some evocation of this illusion—the demoniacal behavior of Ahab in Melville's *Moby Dick*, for instance—usually present or imply an objective, rational, normative, or metaphysical frame of reference which allows the reader to recognize the private aberration for what it is. In the case of Nathan, who often stresses the lonely isolation of each human being and who frequently dramatizes the common illusions of man and society, it seems abundantly clear that adopting pathological illusion as a model for fiction is quite unthinkable. He has little more than polite contempt for any kind of surrealism in the arts.

[146]

Fantasy of Reverie. Pathological fantasy tends to terminate in a private distortion of reality, but literary fantasy seeks to foster new public appreciation of the variety and complexity of reality. Nevertheless, literary fantasy often blends private and public consciousness without becoming pathological. When the average person indulges in moments of free association—eyes ajar, unhearing, apparently unaware of the tangible world around him, but inwardly entranced by some spontaneous rush of secret hopes, half-remembered fears, angers, frustrations, loves, and triumphs all tumbling wildly through his head—we are inclined to excuse his reverie as natural and perhaps wholesome. But such a reverie, if James Harvey Robinson is right in *The Mind in the Making,* is usually a selfish and petty experience in which embarrassingly immature notions flatter the ego. He holds all reverie suspect: "It doubtless influences all our speculations in its persistent tendency to self-magnification and self-justification, which are its chief preoccupations, but it is the last thing to make directly or indirectly for honest increase of knowledge."[8]

Not surprisingly there are several sub-literary kinds of writing which find their formal meaning through imitation of this sane, but quite silly, pattern of reverie. In writing of this sort there is rarely any esthetic distance between the story and reality, so that the reader, far from finding a perspective on life through fiction, is encouraged to identify with some grossly drawn hero who always seems to make his way through a clutter of quasi-realistic trouble by use of violence and charm, with unquestioned right, to some wholly incredible success. Such fiction is the very world of reveries come true. Examples of it are the fantasies written by Hans Christian Anderson, by Owen Wister, and by Edgar Rice Burroughs, as are those illiterate formula-fantasies of sex and sadism purveyed by the non-books and non-films of recent years.

Such uninhibited story-telling fills Nathan with revulsion. He abhors violence. As a child he was frightened, Nathan once said in the course of a television interview,[9] by the harsh implications of *Alice in Wonderland;* upon reading it again some fifty years later, he was still dismayed by the fantasy of violence. The only tale he ever wrote expressly for children, *The Snowflake and the Starfish* (1959), betrays no egoistic or compensatory attitudes in its author and surely does not seem to encourage any in its readers; if anything, the tale suffers from a want of explicit conflict to make its theme clear and memorable. As an adult, he continues to be offended by violence in visceral novels written in the manner of Norman Mailer; he denounces them in his prefatory essays, satirizes them in his fiction, shuns their style in practice. His reaction to ordinary television fare is much the same, as illustrated by random satire in his novel, *The Color of Evening.*

Fantasy of Imagination. Not all reveries are frivolous; what once were daydreams have often matured into an empire across the seas, some new axis of science, or a fresh nexus of art. When reverie is incorporated into a work of art, however, it becomes part of some conscious design. If it still evokes a sense of irrationality, dwells in self-obsession, or exploits the secret hungers of man—as indeed it may—that reverie is no longer so important as a private entity; it serves instead to define some part of a larger public meaning implicit or explicit in the total work, as in James Thurber's story about "The Secret Life of Walter Mitty," or as in William Faulkner's frequent use of multiple reveries to suggest a complex social, temporal, spatial, and psychological conception.

Thus far in the discussion we have been most concerned with varieties of psychological fantasy. But it is inappropriate to describe the fantasy found in literature exclusively in such terms; in fact, it soon becomes awkward to think of fantasy in terms of any rigid criteria, so various are its forms and functions. Certainly E. M. Forster showed an acute diffidence about defining fantasy as a distinct literary genre. In *Aspects of the Novel* he lists some of the similarities often noted in works called *fantasy*, but he is especially careful to point out that fantasy means many things to many people. "It implies the supernatural," he says, "but need not express it. Often it does express it, and were that type of classification helpful, we could make a list of the devices which writers of a fantastic turn have used—such as the introduction of a god, ghost, angel, monkey, monster, midget, witch into ordinary life; of the introduction of ordinary men into no man's land, the future, the past, the interior of the earth, the fourth dimension; of divings into and dividings of personality; or finally the device of parody or adaptation."[10]

Nathan employs most of these fantastic devices at one time or another in his fiction. God has a speaking role in *Jonah* and in *Mr. Whittle and the Morning Star;* angels, demons, and demi-spirits of various kinds are also introduced into stories ostensbily concerned with ordinary life. In addition there are worldly dogs, philosophical horses, communistic ants, capitalistic cockroaches, a sea-witch lover, an insecure fox, a narcissistic whale, and sundry other creatures who sometimes converse easily with the human beings in the fiction and who at other times occupy a separate but equal world of their own.

Ordinary men, on the other hand, are introduced into bizarre circumstances, and without the least apology, to prowl about heaven, live in successive generations, disport with Neanderthals, bargain with demons, or confer with God as occasion permits. The fantasy of time and space, suggestive of a fourth dimension, is a basic element in several of Nathan's novels. At least once, in *The Wilderness Stone,* he experiments with a divided personality as he tries to bring his own New York years into stereoptic focus. *Autumn* is an adaptation of *The Little Flowers of Saint Francis; Jonah* is a redaction of the famous biblical prophecy. Ancient folklore provides the myth of *So Love Returns; The Devil* with *Love* is a parody in earnest of the Faust legend.

But to name instances in this fashion is not to consider function and effect. Nathan's fantasy at its best is a displacement by which he makes biblical myth and metaphor serve his interest in contemporary secular life. *Autumn* serves as an example. If Americans will no longer heed the mystical instruction of Saint Francis, will they perhaps respond to his simple plea for universal love and piety if the medieval sermons-in-story are shifted to a New England setting with a country schoolmaster in the holy father's role? This novel not only transposes a medieval "world view" into contemporary Vermont; it also converts all actors in the familiar allegory into caricature types of the modern American. This deliberate displacement exposes each realm of experience to fresh examination in a new perspective.

Actually, Nathan's *Jonah* is a more successful example of literary displacement; for, even though the author retains the major figures, time, events, and geography relatively intact, he extrapolates in such a way that a modern dimension is added to the spare old prophecy. He introduces a whole community of ordinary human beings; gives a dissenting voice to the great fish; adds creatures of earth, demons of the netherworld, and saints from heaven. And, by their personal and social involvement, he manages to create additional levels of meaning not even touched upon in the original, where merely personal and social considerations are subordinate to spiritual obligation. Nevertheless, this displacement helps to make the ancient myth meaningful to modern man, if only because he sees his secular interests duly reflected in the fuller account of young Jonah's career.

The Bishop's Wife, for all its chic urbanity, is at bottom very like the old temptation of Adam; in this instance, however, the angel Michael plays the male lead; and, because he is more than willing to succumb to female charm himself, the story seems to suggest that Adam's behavior might have some excuse. This novel illustrates displacement of time, place, and major characters in order to invite fresh consideration of a story first told in Genesis. Some Christians think the story is a divine indictment of human carnality, most Jews reject such an allegorical interpretation, but Nathan takes no side in that controversy. He is not trying to discredit the truth behind any myth he examines; he seeks instead to demonstrate that the truth is greater than the historical myths which attempt to define it.

There Is Another Heaven makes clear that one need not be a Moses in order to feel like smashing idols; *One More Spring* evokes the ancient sense of charity; *Road of Ages* demonstrates the patience man must learn in suffering; *Portrait of Jennie* suggests how mortal love may grow into immortal understanding; *Mr. Whittle and the Morning Star* finds in our nuclear predicament all the elements of a last judgment; and *A Star in the Wind* is the story of everyman searching always for the promised land.

The works of fantasy in which Nathan adapts ancient stories for a modern audience, or displaces biblical mythology to serve as a contemporary frame of reference, and thus permit a running critique of current experience within a larger and older perspective, often have a homely and humanistic bias. But there is also a spiritual dimension to Nathan's imagination—something intuitive, supernatural, and mysterious. "Sooner or later," according to his indirect testimony in *Portrait of Jennie*, "God asks His question: are you for me, or against me? And the artist must have some answer, or feel his heart break for what he cannot say" (5).

In the more direct testimony of his fictionized autobiography, *The Wilderness Stone*, he tries to describe the transcendental importance of human imagination. "When I speak of the imagination," says the older of his alter egos in the story,

I am not speaking of memory, of those horrors or delicacies put together out of travel books and fears, old tales and dragon's blood, Lucifer, legend, and photographs of the moon. I am talking about something as pure as mathematics or ice water. I believe it to be man's soul, the only thing he has freed of the complaining flesh. Somehow in the universe, somewhere in the imagination, is God; and imagination searches Him out. (50)

VI   *A Wizard Does Things with the Heart*

Nathan's short novel *Stonecliff* (1967) provides a case study in fiction of the writer's involvement in the creative process that results in a fantasy based on feeling. One fictional pattern in the book tends to be a public, quasi-biographical, and relatively explicit account of the "sorcery" practiced by Edward Granville, novelist in his late sixties, who is currently at work on his thirty-second novel, and who has a house guest, Michael Robb, a young critic come to interview the long-established if recently neglected novelist in order to write his biography. Another fictional pattern in the book tends to be a private, quasi-autobiographical, and never more than implicit account of Nathan's own literary method. Both patterns are defined by a single story in which characters and events have multiple significance.

Granville (a mask for Nathan) is not too sure that Robb (who may represent Nathan's uncomprehending critics)[11] will ever fully understand that the "true sorcerer deals with illusion" and that his art "does things to the heart" (27); he nevertheless permits the young man to stay and watch how his magic—which is not so different actually from the magic employed by Shakespeare's Prospero—can indeed evoke feelings which seem to open into fresh dimensions of human understanding.

The novelist explains that he cannot write except when he himself is in love (102), so he has conjured up the living memory of his wife Virginia Granville (a mask for Nathan's present wife, Shirley Kneeland Nathan) as she was when first they fell in love. The original Virginia, a vital lady of sixty, has thus been transformed by the author's imagination into a girl who represents the fresh essence of young love and who does inspire her husband to create once more a world of enchantment. Stephen Vincent Benét was once inspired, Granville says, to just this sort of creative sorcery by the love of his wife Rosemary (26).

Robb seems unaware that by sharing Granville's imaginative

world he may also fall under the artist's spell, and may even be used by a writer who uses everything (15). So when Robb meets Nina, the young girl that Granville has conjured up for inspiration, the young man not only fails to guess that she is really Virginia Granville, but also falls in love with her. He thus becomes a victim of illusion induced by art that does things to his heart. If Granville is not much surprised by the young man's passionate interest in Nina—and the novelist does explain, after all, that he typically creates a girl only he can see at first, but that he knows other people will see and love her too when they enter his enchanted realm of imagination (14)—he is nevertheless troubled by the threat youth always seems to pose for age.

The central problem explored in *Stonecliff*, as a matter of fact, is our perennial puzzle about man and God, particularly as that mystery influences our illusions about youth and age and love. This often results, Granville thinks, in an open contest between youth and age (123); and sometimes the contest develops curious problems for the artist. Even the fictional Max Loeb, for example, an aging painter created in Granville's work-in-progress (which we recognize as Nathan's 1960 novel, *The Color of Evening*), is most unhappily involved in such a contest with his protégé Jon because they both love the girl called Halys; moreover, since Granville simply puts down his fictional characters as best he can in flesh and blood, and then lets their own natures draw them to their destiny (152), the character called Max Loeb actually comes to argue with Granville about the role he feels the author is imposing on him (86), complaining most that Granville makes him struggle for love he cannot hope to have (88) since he obviously is no young lion (89). And Granville understands full well this character's frustration in contending with youth; was Granville not tempted, on one occasion (135), to impale young Robb upon a javelin?

As usual in a fantasy by Nathan, the basic mysteries are not solved but the surface conflicts are reconciled. Granville finally releases his wife Virginia from her role as the ingénue called Nina, and from the embarrassment of being the focus in a contest between age and youth, for the novelist manages to finish his book and presumably can get along on the conventional inspiration of mature married love. He also settles his feud with Max Loeb, at the same time, and grants this character the peace of sensible surrender in his separate contest with youth within the pages of fiction. Meanwhile young Robb has become conscious of the illusions and implications in Granville's imaginative world, not all of which he understands; yet he does end up at last "half-believing the unbelievable" (164), and doubtless recognizes the premises underlying Granville's fantasy of feeling: that art is never divorced from life, that tangible forms have no more reality than the configurations of imagination, that rationality is in no way superior to feeling, and that the mystery suggested by all the illusions generated by art and life actually represents the enormous symbiosis of a divine imagination. Hence any approach to art, young Robb seems entitled to infer, which purports to interpret it in purely logical fashion, or which fails to emphasize the artist's biography and subjective convictions, may result in sterile criticism quite unsuited to the task of discovering the mode and meaning of fantasy based on feeling.

VII *Conclusion*

Nathan's characteristic premises are conservative, his literary patterns are frequently adaptations of familiar forms, his verbal texture preserves much of the language and tropes of Judeo-Christian tradition, his pervasive tone is less satirical than ironic—and less ironic than anagogical. His literary achievement assures him of a place in the goodly company of American popular writers.

To say that Nathan's characteristic premises are conservative we must make an oversimple distinction in the manner of T. E. Hulme, who divides all modern writers into mutually exclusive categories, one composed of those who have a Romantic view of man—the individual—as an infinite reservoir of possibilities, and the other composed of those who have a Classical view of man as an extraordinarily fixed and limited animal whose nature is absolutely constant and whose only decent achievement depends on support from tradition and organization.[12] And a casual inspection of Nathan's work may not suggest that he belongs in fact among the conservatives, for certainly his fantasies present wholesome (if confused) protagonists in decent (if troubled) human circumstances, and their problems are usually treated with sympathy and resolved by a happy ending. But these heroes persist—they do not prevail; and the happy endings are specious devices intended to comfort those whom Nathan fears may be appalled by truth.[18] Yet that truth, or so much of it as the author thinks he recognizes, is never concealed. In book after book the protagonists who speak or meditate about the major themes are unanimous in saying that man is actually ignorant, savage, fearful, and cruel at heart and therefore desperately needs the sort of guidance offered by the traditions of Christian love, Jewish piety, and Roman Stoicism if he hopes to survive the chaos of contemporary anomie.

Nathan's structural concepts also tend to be conservative; his literary patterns are frequently adaptations of familiar forms. Of course the richness of his fantasy is prima facie evidence of the author's power of invention; and certainly Nathan can manipulate a reader's dearest confidence in such things as time, identity, function, and significance with both droll and devastating effect. Nevertheless, the basic story frames on which he stretches his fabrications are often refurbished folk tales, myths, biblical episodes, and allegories known to young and old for generations. More often than not, his stories are actually shaped by the ancient and recurrent human situations they reproduce; and then, in lieu of conventional plot or character development, his fiction generates another sort of drama by gradually reminding us of the abiding beauty, the certain pain, the perennial seasons of joy, and the endless mystery of this human adventure which we are prone to take for granted. The fresh angles of vision provided by the displacements wrought by fantasy always come into a familiar focus on our unchanging human condition.

The verbal texture of Nathan's most characteristic work is especially redolent of the past. The vocabulary he employs in verse and in the prose meditations scattered through all his novels tends to parallel or repeat the simple, pastoral, earthbound, nature-loving, sky-mystified, and God-intoxicated language of biblical prophecy and poetry. The tropes he uses to suggest the ineffable nature of God may baffle or provoke some modern readers, for the anti-intellectual mysticism they deliberately invoke has been quite out of style in Western civilization since the Middle Ages, if we care to take Henry Adams as our authority.[14] But even modern readers can surely appreciate how the rhythm and repetend employed in Nathan's best verse suggest the old magic of the Psalms, and how the great cadences of nature imagery in his prose meditations echo if they cannot duplicate the thunder of ancient prophecy.

As a matter of fact, the most pervasive tone running through Nathan's work is anagogical—a term meant to suggest the attitude of mystical and transcendental wonder the author adopts toward every subject he seriously considers, whether that subject be an ant, a nebula, a man, or the pure stuff of imagination. In the early fiction, to be sure, his emphasis is more humanistic than theistic; God is then his trouble, mortality his privilege, and freckled human nature his exasperated concern in fiction that runs heavily to satire. In the novels of his middle years Nathan's ridicule mellows steadily into sympathy, and even when he treats such things as the terror of genocide his work is much less satirical than ironic. But in his latest books the hope for man is almost gone, and his fiction grows still more sober and mystical in developing major themes; *A Star in the Wind* (1962) makes human tradition, love, and patience seem no more than variant forms of a larger piety imposed by the mystery of being. Of course all these attitudes are present to some degree in every book from *Peter Kindred* (1920) to *Stonecliff* (1967); but the earliest serious tone, and the one that finally dominates all others, can only be described as anagogical.

Within such a world of transcendental mystery we are not surprised to find that the personae of Nathan's imaginative works are usually archetypes. They are certainly not heroes or villains in the conventional sense, for such roles presume a personal significance and competence the author does not attribute to any mortal creature. His most memorable characters—wretched human exiles, worldly dogs, lovable Shlemihls, idyllic lovers, the combatants in an average marriage, and various lonely human beings obsessed by the mystery of God—do indeed have functional parts, but they are archetypal, and not unique; in an ultimate sense they prove to be no more than multiple definitions of one consistent human nature which they can neither fully understand or modify. They are all God's sparrows, but ignorant of His inscrutable purpose.

In writing for a popular audience, Nathan tends to clarify those ideas which are already in circulation, to evoke those feelings people are ready to accept, to "explain" complex problems in oversimple terms, or by reductive arguments, or by unqualified appeals to historical precedent or to ancient but surviving custom, and to include too much "escapist" entertainment in his serious work; but while Nathan does indeed try to engage popular interest he does not cater to the gross aspects of popular taste, and vehemently opposes the cults of literary violence which appear to exploit human weakness.[15] Nathan's literary achievement can therefore be described as a reassertion of the dignity and importance of the genuinely popular writer, who may very well rely upon conservative premises, familiar forms, traditional language and tropes, a frankly mystical tone, and archetypal characters in order to produce fresh works of ancient wonder that everyone can read with pleasure and profit, but who is just as anxious as any writer in the *avant garde* to discover and assert the civilized consensus in which Western man may find the good, the true, and the beautiful.

His best work begins in pleasure and ends in piety. *Jonah* (1925) has urbanity and wit, which is expressed in a prose style equal to that of Washington Irving, yet concludes in serious speculation about the nature of religious sensibility. *The Bishop's Wife* (1928) sparkles with the irony of human and angelic misconceptions, yet it avoids the religious scepticism found in similar works by Anatole France; and *There Is Another Heaven* (1929) abounds with caustic satire of man's celestial illusions, yet it nowhere betrays the bitter disillusionment found in Mark Twain's later speculation about our human destiny. *Road of Ages* (1935) evokes pity and terror by its depiction of man's inhumanity to man, and does not blanch at offering instances of macabre comedy, yet it shuns the terrible conclusions found in George Orwell's fictional prediction of the future; and *Portrait of Jennie* (1940) conjures up the American dream of romantic love in all of its shivering wonder, yet it declines to operate within the simply mortal limits of similar stories by Thomas Wolfe. Nathan's fiction nearly always includes a spiritual emphasis that permits his humor and ridicule to open a way to hope and faith.

Of course some of his most charming work originates in secular concern and dramatizes our mortality. "Dunkirk" (1941) is the sort of patriotic ballad John Greenleaf Whittier or Henry Wadsworth Longfellow might well have written had they known the dark days of World War II. *Morning in Iowa* (1944) is a narrative in verse that succeeds in its frank imitation of Stephen Vincent Benét's nostalgic celebration of the American dream. *The Innocent Eve* (1951), Nathan's most trenchant satire, is an allegorical fantasy about our modern efforts to establish nuclear control that invites comparison with some of Nathaniel Hawthorne's dark tales of human perversity; and *Jezebel's Husband* (1953), Nathan's most successful play to date, is a situation comedy based on that old battle of the sexes also treated, but seldom with more humor, by James Thurber. *Sir Henry* (1955) is both deft and daft, one of the author's happiest achievements in droll fantasy, complete with talking animals, a lovable old Shlemihl in rusting armor, and two vaporous maidens who all fall within a farce but who survive in the reader's sympathy; briefer in scope, less structured in design and argument, this short novel is nevertheless equal to the best of James Branch Cabell's fantasies, perhaps because it has the wit one might expect if Robert Benchley had helped Nathan invent the incidents. *So Love Returns* (1958) is the adaptation of an old folk legend, and both in mood and manner it reminds us of the graceful fables Washington Irving resurrected in Germany which are also half witchcraft and half truth.

A Star in the Wind (1962), a full-length novel devoid of fantasy, has unique power in suggesting the interior crisis a perennial exile suffers in renouncing familiar ties in order to help create a new homeland; as it happens this story of the effort to create modern Israel often lacks the overt conflict, complex detail, and social immediacy found, for example, in the novel Leon Uris wrote on the same subject; but Nathan is more successful in evoking the timeless quality of the Jewish struggle and in suggesting the internal complications of a man swept along by ancient destiny.

In this brief recitation of some of Nathan's most distinctive literary accomplishments he has frequently been compared to other authors who addressed a popular audience, and these comparisons have been anything but accidental. He shares with them an interest in the average man in ordinary life, and this interest is important today. For in an age of personal alienation and social dysfunction, when the mass media seldom deal in anything but persiflage and child-oriented entertainments, and when the elite arts seem so intent on complexity and repudiation that they often become unintelligible or unconvincing to most general readers, the elemental grace and decency of Nathan's art and the probity of his familiar argument afford precisely that stabilizing influence the mass of men seem to require in times of change.

Notes and References

Chapter One

1. Nathan's recollection of the publication date proves inexact. His meticulous bibliographer, Dan H. Laurence, explains in *Robert Nathan: A Bibliography* (New Haven, 1960) that *Peter Kindred* was actually entered for copyright on January 21, 1920, and that an edition of one thousand copies was published on January 21, 1920, two copies of which were deposited in the Library of Congress on January 31, 1920.

2. This summary indictment represents the cumulative judgment of the contributors to *Civilization in the United States: An Inquiry by Thirty Americans,* edited by Harold Stearns (New York, 1922).

3. Eliot G. Fay, "Borrowings from Anatole France by Willa Cather and Robert Nathan," *Modern Language Review* (May, 1941), p. 377.

4. Robert Nathan, *The Concert* (New York, 1940), pp. 7-8. This small clothbound book, with only thirty pages of text, comprises the first two chapters of the substantially unpublished manuscript entitled *The Letters of Fra Rombadille.*

5. Robert Nathan, "This Thing Called Art," *Reviewer* (November, 1921), pp. 87-89.

6. Robert Nathan, "Peter Truffle Meditates," *Reviewer* (April, 1922), pp. 404-5.

7. Paraphrased from *A Treasury of Yiddish Stories* by Irving Howe and Eliezer Greenberg. Copyright 1953, 1954 by The Viking Press, Inc. All Rights Reserved. Reprinted by permission of The Viking Press, Inc.

Chapter Two

1. The verse is untitled in its first appearance in *Autumn* (16-17); it is one of four brief songs included in the text of that novel. As reprinted in *A Cedar Box* (1929) the verse is retitled "Text in Economics"; and as reprinted in *The Green Leaf: The Collected Poems of Robert Nathan* (1950) the verse serves as the first of four quatrains in an expanded version of the original theme under the general title of "Two Texts in Economics" (111).

2. Robert Nathan, "On Being a Jew," *Scribner's,* XCIII (June, 1933), pp. 372-73.

3. Although a distinction is sometimes made between the *Shlemihl*

(the dope) and the *Shlimazl* (the hard-luck guy), as in the popular anecdote where the Shlemihl spills hot soup on the best pants of the Shlimazl, this distinction is not used in the present study. Nathan's characters are seldom without some blame for their own misfortune. For a fuller discussion of this character type consult Theodor Reik, *Jewish Wit* (New York, 1962).

4. Edith McEwen Dorian, "While a Little Dog Dances—Robert Nathan: Novelist of Simplicity," *The Sewanee Review* (Spring, 1933), p. 129.

5. Paraphrased from *A Treasury of Yiddish Stories* by Irving Howe and Eliezer Greenberg. Copyright 1953, 1954 by The Viking Press, Inc. All Rights Reserved. Reprinted by permission of The Viking Press, Inc.

Chapter Three

1. *The Green Leaf*, p. 136.

2. Dr. Edmund Bergler, in *Laughter and the Sense of Humor* (New York, 1956), sees psychic masochism at work in the recital of personal shortcomings which he finds characteristic in Jewish wit (112).

3. Theodor Reik reviews the general problem of Jewish self-degradation in *Jewish Wit* (New York, 1962), pp. 219-26.

4. Susanne K. Langer, *Philosophy in a New Key: A Study in the Symbolism of Reason, Rite, and Art* (Cambridge, 1957), pp. 28 ff.

5. Kathleen Nott, *The Emperor's Clothes* (Bloomington, 1958), p. 21.

6. In the course of an interview Nathan confirmed that credulous readers of *Portrait of Jennie* applied in such numbers at the Metropolitan Museum of Art to inspect the alleged portrait the novel said was hanging there that the museum staff finally obliged by displaying an approximation.

7. Laura Krey, "Time and the English Novel," *Twentieth Century English,* edited by W. S. Knickerbocker (New York, 1946), pp. 401-15.

Chapter Four

1. Robert Nathan, "A Novelist Looks at Hollywood," *Hollywood Quarterly* (January, 1946), pp. 146-47.

2. Edmund Carpenter, "Our New Languages, The Mass Media," *Explorations,* No.7 (March, 1957), pp. 4-21.

3. Intended to serve as an introduction to the book version of *Bridgit* (a motion picture scenario that was not produced), the essay attempts to show the general reader how a writer functions in Hollywood.

4. Based on one of several interviews Nathan granted the author during preparation of this study.

5. James Agee, *Agee on Film: Reviews and Comment* (New York, 1958), pp. 164-65.

6. Quotations on pp. 85 and 86 are based on one of several interviews of the author with Nathan.

7. Letter to John Fall, in Nathan Manuscript Collection, Yale University Library.

Chapter Five

1. Reprinted in *The Green Leaf*, p. 76.
2. *Ibid.*, p. 159.
3. *Ibid.*, p. 123.
4. *Ibid.*, p. 161.
5. *Ibid.*, p. 138.
6. *Ibid.*, p. 38.
7. Based on one of several interviews Nathan granted the author during preparation of this study.
8. See, for example, the opening lines of Stephen Vincent Benét's "American Names," which is included in *Selected Works of Stephen Vincent Benét* (New York, 1953).
9. Reprinted in *The Green Leaf*, pp. 6-9.
10. *Ibid.*, p. 145.
11. *Ibid.*, p. 77.
12. *Ibid.*, p. 177.
13. *Ibid.*, p. 28.
14. *Ibid.*, p. 112.
15. *Ibid.*, pp. 13-14.
16. *Ibid.*, p. 118.
17. *Ibid.*, p. 116.
18. *Ibid.*, p. 136.
19. *Ibid.*, p. 149.
20. *Ibid.*, p. 19.
21. *Ibid.*, p. 135.
22. *Ibid.*, p. 150.
23. *Ibid.*, pp. 182-83.
24. *Ibid.*, p. 146.

Chapter Six

1. Reprinted in *The Green Leaf*, p. 95.
2. *Ibid.*, p. 96.
3. *Ibid.*, p. 18.
4. *Ibid.*, p. 23.

5. *Ibid.*, p. 131.

6. Father Myers of Saint Francis Xavier Parish in Burbank, California, recommends a free translation of the Latin passage used by Nathan:

"We exorcise you," he cried, "all unclean spirits, all Satanic powers, all accursed and infernal adversaries, all legions, all diabolical congregations and sects, in the name and by the virtue of our Lord"—here he made the sign of the Cross—"Christ; be purged and flee from the Church of God and from the spirit and image of God represented by the precious and redemptive blood of the divine Lamb"—

7. See Susanne K. Langer, *Philosophy in a New Key* (Cambridge, 1942), p. 15.

Chapter Seven

1. *The Green Leaf*, p. 99.
2. *Ibid.*, p. 150.
3. *Ibid.*, p. 67.
4. Based on one of several interviews Nathan granted the author during preparation of this study.
5. Northrop Frye, "The Mythos of Winter: Irony and Satire," in his *Anatomy of Criticism* (Princeton, 1957), pp. 223-39.
6. *The Green Leaf*, p. 139.
7. C. S. Lewis, "The Meanings of Fantasy," in his *An Experiment in Criticism* (Cambridge, 1961), pp. 50-56.
8. John Harvey Robinson, "On Various Kinds of Thinking," in his *The Mind in the Making* (New York, 1921), p. 2.
9. Nathan appeared on an educational television program with the author in March, 1960, and discussed various aspects of fantasy using *Alice in Wonderland* as a major point of reference.
10. E. M. Forster, *Aspects of the Novel* (New York, 1927), p. 165.
11. *Stonecliff* (1967) was written more than a year after Nathan completed the interviews with the author of this study. In the course of those interviews, as he expressed it, he had ample opportunity to recall how his work had been received by the public and by critics, and to reflect on the basic premises his books employ and endorse. And since Nathan makes a practice of transforming his actual experience into fiction—as the characters of *Stonecliff* are made to say repeatedly (15, 47, 48)—it should prove no surprise for us to find *Stonecliff* deals with the issues raised by various critics. Nathan humorously identifies his novel as a weapon in the steady duel he has with them (82).

Some reviewers and critics have indeed said that Nathan relies excessively on nostalgia, escape, or sentiment, but Granville (a mask for Nathan) makes no explicit reference to such cavils. He does seem to acknowledge, however, the possibility of our misconstruing his hopeful bias insinuated by happy endings. He admits that human beings can only remember part of the past, and that our youth may have been less gay than we now recall it (23); he also concedes, in any event, that we cannot go back into the past (77). Granville is equally explicit in repudiating the notion that love is eternal (109, 146), and that there is, indeed, no real escape from loneliness so far as he can see (148). To the degree that Granville does speak for Nathan, these various remarks are worth considering in any serious appraisal of such books as *Autumn, One More Spring,* or *Portrait of Jennie,* where just such qualifications may prove desirable.

Of the reviewers who had occasion to discuss *Stonecliff* following its appearance, it is interesting to notice that very few showed the perspicacity of Robert K. Kirsch, whose notice in the Los Angeles *Times* (March 19, 1967) treated the serious esthetic implications woven into Nathan's fantasy.

12. T. E. Hulme, "Romanticism and Classicism," in his *Speculations* (New York, 1924).

13. Based on one of several interviews of the author with Nathan.

14. In *Mont-Saint-Michel and Chartres* Henry Adams makes his familiar remark that any man who wonders into the eleventh century is lost, unless he can grow prematurely young (2).

15. See, for example, Nathan's "A Note to the Younger Generation" in his *The Barly Fields: A Collection of Five Novels* (New York, 1938).

Selected Bibliography

Bibliography

Dan H. Laurence, *Robert Nathan: A Bibliography*. New Haven, Yale University Press, 1960.

PRIMARY SOURCES

1. *Books, Pamphlets*

Peter Kindred. New York: Duffield and Company, 1919 (Actually published 1920). A novel.

Autumn. New York: Robert M. McBride & Company, 1921. Short novel.

Youth Grows Old. New York: Robert M. McBride & Company, 1922. Verse.

The Puppet Master. New York: Robert M. McBride & Company, 1923. Short novel.

Jonah. New York: Robert M. McBride & Company, 1925. Short novel.

The Fiddler in Barly. New York: Robert M. McBride & Company, 1926. Short novel.

The Woodcutter's House. Indianapolis: The Bobbs-Merrill Company, 1927. Short novel.

The Bishop's Wife. Indianapolis: The Bobbs-Merrill Company, 1928. Short novel.

A Cedar Box. Indianapolis: The Bobbs-Merrill Company, 1929. Verse.

There Is Another Heaven. Indianapolis: The Bobbs-Merrill Company, 1929. Short novel.

The Orchid. Indianapolis: The Bobbs-Merrill Company, 1931. Short novel.

One More Spring. New York: Alfred A. Knopf, 1933. Short novel.

Road of Ages. New York: Alfred A. Knopf, 1935. Short novel.

Selected Poems of Robert Nathan. New York: Alfred A. Knopf, 1935.

The Enchanted Voyage. New York: Alfred A. Knopf, 1936. Short novel.

Fear Not the Night. San Mateo: Theodore Lilienthal, 1937. Reprinting of verse in limited edition; not for sale.

Winter in April. New York: Alfred A. Knopf, 1938. Short novel.

The Barly Fields: A Collection of Five Novels by Robert Nathan.

Introduction by Stephen Vincent Benét. New York: Alfred A. Knopf, 1938. Contains Nathan's "A Note to the Younger Generation," dated December 1937, and five previously published novels: *The Fiddler in Barly, The Woodcutter's House, The Bishop's Wife, The Orchid, There Is Another Heaven.*

Journey of Tapiola. New York: Alfred A. Knopf, 1938. A very brief novel.

Portrait of Jennie. New York: Alfred A. Knopf, 1940. Short novel.

The Concert. New York: House of Books, Ltd., 1940. Two chapters separately printed from the unpublished novel, *The Letters of Fra Rombadille.*

A Winter Tide: Sonnets & Poems by Robert Nathan. New York: Alfred A. Knopf, 1940.

They Went on Together. New York: Alfred A. Knopf, 1941. Short novel.

Tapiola's Brave Regiment. New York: Alfred A. Knopf, 1941. A very brief novel.

Dunkirk. New York: Alfred A. Knopf, 1941. A ballad of 104 lines separately printed.

The Sea-Gull Cry. New York: Alfred A. Knopf, 1942. Short novel.

Journal for Josephine. New York: Alfred A. Knopf, 1943. Autobiographical reminiscence of World War II years on Cape Cod.

But Gently Day. New York: Alfred A. Knopf, 1943. Short novel.

Morning in Iowa. New York: Alfred A. Knopf, 1944. A verse narrative.

The Darkening Meadows: Poems, Including 'Dunkirk'. New York: Alfred A. Knopf, 1945.

Mr. Whittle and the Morning Star. New York: Alfred A. Knopf, 1947. Short novel.

Long After Summer. New York: Alfred A. Knopf, 1948. Short novel.

The River Journey. New York: Alfred A. Knopf, 1949. Short novel.

The Green Leaf: The Collected Poems of Robert Nathan. New York: Alfred A. Knopf, 1950.

The Married Look. New York: Alfred A. Knopf, 1950. Short novel.

The Adventures of Tapiola. New York: Alfred A. Knopf, 1950. Reprinting of two previously published short novels: *Journey of Tapiola* and *Tapiola's Brave Regiment.*

The Innocent Eve. New York: Alfred A. Knopf, 1951. Short novel.

Nathan 3: The Sea-Gull Cry, The Innocent Eve, The River Journey. London: Staples Press, 1952. Reprinting of previously published short novels.

Jezebel's Husband and *The Sleeping Beauty.* New York: Alfred A. Knopf, 1953. Two plays.

The Train in the Meadow. New York: Alfred A. Knopf, 1953. Short novel.

Selected Bibliography

Sir Henry. New York: Alfred A. Knopf, 1955. Short novel.
The Rancho of Little Loves. New York: Alfred A. Knopf, 1956. Short
    novel.
So Love Returns. New York: Alfred A. Knopf, 1958. Short novel.
The Snowflake and the Starfish. New York: Alfred A. Knopf, 1959.
    A juvenile story.
The Color of Evening. New York: Alfred A. Knopf, 1960. Short novel.
The Weans. New York: Alfred A. Knopf, 1960. Tale of ironic science
    fiction; Nathan classifies it as "Archeology."
The Wilderness-Stone. New York: Alfred A. Knopf, 1961. Short
    novel.
A Star in the Wind. New York: Alfred Knopf, 1962. A novel.
The Married Man. New York: Alfred A. Knopf, 1962. Light verse.
The Devil WITH *Love*. New York: Alfred A. Knopf, 1963. Short novel.
The Fair. New York: Alfred A. Knopf, 1964. Short novel.
The Mallot Diaries. New York: Alfred A. Knopf, 1965. Short novel.
Juliet in Mantua. New York: Alfred A. Knopf, 1966. Play.
Stonecliff. New York: Alfred A. Knopf, 1967. Short novel.

2. *Representative Periodical Pieces by Robert Nathan*:

"It: The Usual Play with an Unusual Ending," *Smart Set* (Decem-
    ber, 1915), 85-90.
"Atavism: A Tale of Passions in the Rough," *Smart Set* (September,
    1916), 197-202.
"This Thing Called Art," *Reviewer* (November, 1921), 87-89.
"The Tragedy of Octave Moll," *Reviewer* (December, 1921), 115-21.
"Peter Truffle Meditates," *Reviewer* (April, 1922), 404-5.
"A Death in the Stadium," *Scribner's* (September, 1927), 367-68.
"Children in Heaven," *The Saturday Review of Literature* (Novem-
    ber 16, 1929), 396-97.
"The Pair of Pants," *Scribner's* (February, 1930), 216-18.
"Pannickin," *New Yorker* (March 21, 1931), 17-19.
"The Grumbach Bill," *New Yorker* (September 26, 1931), 23-24.
"Dr. Stoke's Statue," *New Yorker* (February 11, 1933), 16-17.
"On Being a Jew," *Scribner's* (June, 1933), 372-73.
"A Power Is Needed" (a contribution to a symposium: "Shall We
    Boycott Germany?"), in *Opinion* (September, 1933), 19.
"England, My England," *New Yorker* (April 28, 1934), 36.
"The Chancellor's Plan," *New Yorker* (October 27, 1934), 17.
"The Great Peace, of Mr. Thomas V. Smith," *New Yorker* (Decem-
    ber 22, 1934), 16.
"Fable of the Atheist," *New Yorker* (May 18, 1935), 28.
"The High Hat," *New Yorker* (March 26, 1938), 17-18.
"Home to Truro," *Vogue* (June 1, 1941), 90, 94.

"Stephen Vincent Benét and His America," *Mark Twain Quarterly* (Winter-Spring, 1943-1944), 4-5.

"A Novelist Looks at Hollywood," *Hollywood Quarterly* (January, 1946), 146-47.

"Agreement in Darien," *Screen Writer* (April, 1948), 12-13.

"Judaism and the 'Lost' Intellectuals" (a symposium), in *Jewish Forum* (September, 1952). Robert Nathan's contribution appears on pp. 129-30.

(Letter on History of *Peter Kindred*). Contributed to Hamilton Vaughan Bail's "Harvard Fiction: Some Critical and Biographical Notes," *Proceedings of the American Antiquarian Society* (October, 1958), 302-3.

"A Pride of Carrots" (a television play), in *Fantasy and Science Fiction* (December, 1959), 100-129.

SECONDARY SOURCES

No attempt has been made to list the several reviews which attended publication of each new book by Nathan; consult *Book Review Digest* for such listings.

Benét, Stephen Vincent. "The World of Robert Nathan." Introduction, *The Barly Fields: A Collection of Five Novels by Robert Nathan*. New York: Alfred A. Knopf, 1938. Brief but suggestive.

Dorian, Edith McEwen, "While a Little Dog Dances—Robert Nathan: Novelist of Simplicity," *The Sewanee Review* (Spring, 1933), 129-40.

Emerson, Dorothy, "Robert Nathan," *Scholastic* (May 2, 1936), 9.

Fay, Eliot G., "Borrowings from Anatole France by Willa Cather and Robert Nathan," *Modern Language Notes* (May, 1941), 377.

Hatcher, Harlan. "Fantasy as a Way of Escape." *Creating the Modern Novel*. New York: Russell & Russell, Inc., 1935. Treats only earlier works, and then only in brief fashion; comments perceptive and just.

Tapley, Roberts, "Robert Nathan: Poet and Ironist," *The Bookman* (October, 1932), 607-14.

Trachtenberg, Stanley, "Robert Nathan's Fiction" (doctoral dissertation, New York University, 1963). The ablest literary critique to date.

Index

Francis of Assisi, 8, 33-37, 52, 149
Freud, Sigmund, 24
Frost, Robert, 19
Frye, Northrup, 140

Gallico, Paul, 82, 83
Galsworthy, John, 7
Gaynor, Janet, 16, 84
Gershwin, George, 53
Goldwyn, Samuel, 85
Grant, Cary, 15, 85
Greenberg, Eliezer, 158
Greene, Graham, 65-66
Greenwich Village, 15, 23, 29
Greenwood, Charlotte, 16
Gulliver's Travels, 27

The Hairy Ape, 36
Harte, Bret, 8
Harvard Monthly, 15
Harvard University, 15, 21, 25, 26
Hatcher, Harlan, 166
Haver, June, 16
Hawthorne, Nathaniel, 19, 156
Hecht, Ben, 20
Hemingway, Ernest, 19, 20, 110
L'Histoire Comique, 33
Hitler, Adolph, 61, 92, 131, 138
Hollywood, 79-86
Hovey, Richard, 24
Howe, Irving, 30, 51
Hulme, T. E., 153, 162
Humor, 39, 40, 45-46, 48, 60, 77, 88, 89, 93, 126, 132, 140-41, 145
Huntington Hartford Foundation, 7

Imagination, 33, 150-51. See also: Fantasy
Irony, 7, 41, 62, 110, 130, 142-45
Irving, Washington, 8, 156, 157
Israel, 17, 111-21

Jeremiah, 62
Jews, 22-23, 29-31, 39-44, 51-52, 55-58, 60-63, 88-90, 110-21, 131, 136. See also: Personae
Job, 143
Jones, Jennifer, 16, 85
Joyce, James, 8, 78
Jung, Carl G., 133

Kafka, Franz, 78, 146
Keel, Howard, 82
Kilmer, Joyce, 24
Kirsch, Robert K., 162
Koster, Bobby, 86
Krey, Laura, 159

Langer, Susanne K., 62, 159
Laurence, Dan H., 9
Lehmann, Lotte, 82
Lewis, C. S., 66, 146, 161
Lewis, Sinclair, 8, 36, 50
Lindbergh, Charles, 53
Lippmann, Walter, 21
The Little Flowers of St. Francis, 33
Longfellow, Henry Wadsworth, 24, 33, 131, 156
Lorenzini, Carlos, 37
Lost generation, 20
Love: thematic definition, 134-39; man and woman, 29, 39, 45, 46, 54-55, 56, 57, 58, 65-74, 77, 93, 95, 104, 109, 120; man and mankind, 34, 35, 64, 86; man and nature, 43, 145; man and the mysteries of death, immortality, and God, 65-74, 95, 121, 123, 125, 136, 152. See also: Personae, Premises

Mailer, Norman, 148
Mann, Thomas, 78
Le Mannequin d'osier, 25
Materialism, 20, 27, 34-36, 37, 50, 58, 60
Medievalism, 32-37, 48
Melville, Herman, 19
Mercer, Jonny, 87
Metro-Goldwyn-Mayer, 79, 80
Metropolitan Museum of Art, 70, 159
Meyer, Anne (Nathan), 15
Michaels, Dorothy, 21
Miller, Arthur, 84
Minelli, Vincent, 82, 83
Mood: the man of feeling, 22, 23, 24, 26, 28, 29, 51-52, 62, 82-83, 130, 151-53; social disillusionment, 23, 36, 53, 59, 93-108, 110-111, 125. See also: Tone

Date Due